RESURRECTION

RESURRECTION

RETURNING TO ROOTS FROM TRAUMA

CJ DAVIS

First Printing, 2023

TO MY PARENTS:

THANK YOU FOR ALWAYS BELIEVING IN ME.

TO MY FRIENDS:

THANK YOU FOR BELIEVING ME.

PATIENT REPORT

PATIENT: DAVIS, CJ

SEX: FEMALE **DATE OF BIRTH:** [***REDACTED***]

ETHNICITY: HISPANIC, INDIGENOUS, WHITE

BACKGROUND: FIRST GEN MEXICAN AMERICAN, GREW UP ATTENDING A CHRISTIAN CHURCH, BORN AND RAISED IN VIRGINIA, CURRENTLY ATTENDS UNIVERSITY

MEDICAL HISTORY: DIAGNOSED WITH BIPOLAR 2 WITH PSYCHOTIC TENDENCIES AT 18

DIAGNOSIS: POST TRAUMATIC STRESS DISORDER

TREATMENT: ART AND WRITING

PROGRESS NOTE: READY TO SHARE HER STORY.

I, __CJ DAVIS__, CONSENT TO SHARING MY SPECIFIC DIAGNOSES MENTIONED ABOVE AND TELLING MY STORY. I PROMISE TO TELL MY TRUTH. I WILL COMPLY WITH MY TREATMENT PLAN.

X__*CJ Davis*____

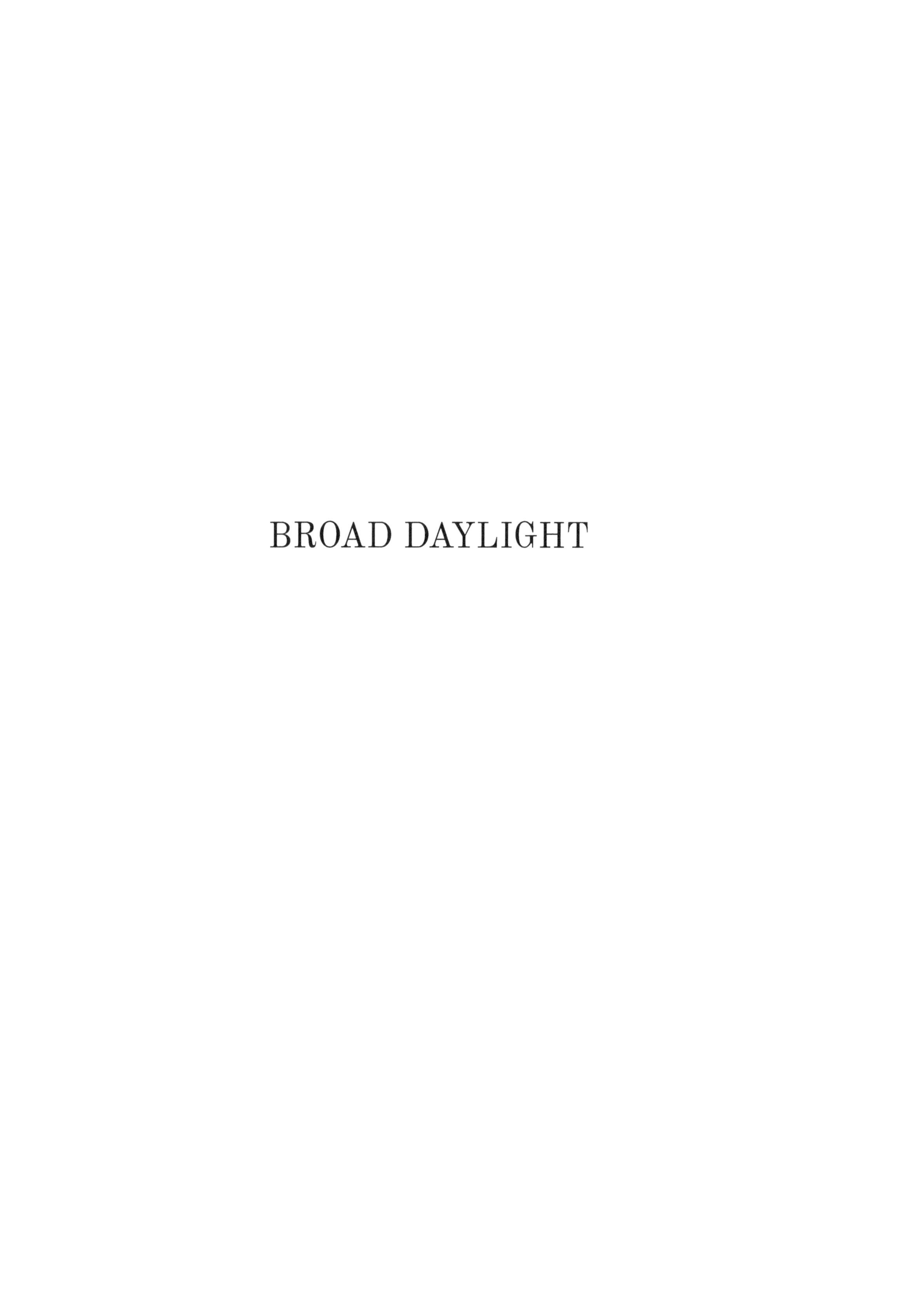

BROAD DAYLIGHT

The Devil Comes in Broad Daylight

If Jesus comes in the middle of the night,
The devil comes in broad daylight.
If the road to heaven if a long narrow road,
the path to hell is a playground slide into sharp mulch
and eternal damnation.
The devil comes in broad daylight and sweeps you away.
Charismatic and young, handsome and unsuspecting.
A slow crawl across the fun monkey bars, up the castle tower,
then the quick slide into hell.
When it was fun, you were young. When you scraped
your knee, your mother put a band aid on it.
When you fell and broke your arm, no one was there,
and the devil was the bully that pushed you down.
You trusted him. In broad daylight.
But...
Jesus comes in the middle of the night.

In the beginning, there was light. Well, it was the bright July sun illuminating a lush green field in front of the decaying columns at the National Arboretum in Washington, DC. I felt warm, 19 years old with the feeling of freedom and the antsy butterflies of new potential. He was a quiet, calm force, that was there in broad daylight, 22 years old with an unbeknownst history.

However, I did not know how turbulent his soul was.

If Jesus comes like a thief in the night, the devil walks in broad daylight.

That was the first date.

There were more dates. After the second it was official, I had a boyfriend. I was a little thrown off by the speed, but at 19 years old with PTSD, when someone tells you they love you, you cling on to every little bit you can get. It started so fast, red flags seem like red hearts when you're speeding through relationship milestones.

By October, I had a promise ring on my left hand ring finger, and I thought that it was normal for someone to want to spend forever with me after about 2 months. The clinginess was flattering, because I never thought someone would love me. I always flashed back to 8th grade, when my best friend stood in front of a crowd, and told me that no one would ever love me, and I would die alone. At 14 years old, my self esteem never hit such a low.

However, my dad always said that there are worse things than being alone. I did not believe him until I suffered through 11 months of 'worse things'. These worse things led to more worse things, and I lost myself.

How do we discern truth when we are lost in the labyrinths of our own realities?

How do we return to our roots when we have lost all hope?

At 21 years old, I picked up a paintbrush again after swearing off of it at age 20, right as I was in the middle of the storm with *him*. I had always drawn, making sure I picked up a pen at least once a day since I was 12, even if it was abstract lines on a napkin.

The brush strokes hit the canvas with such freedom and expression. I could see colors again. The subtle oranges that bring out the blues, the rich yellows that I paired with the lush purples. I had been free from *him* for 7 months at this point, and after the first 5 months of distraught agony, I had felt free.

For the first 5 months of the distraught agony, I had written to keep me sane. I returned to my roots of writing. I had promised my grandmother that I would. 2 weeks before she passed, she could not remember anyone's name, however, when I walked into her room, she pointed at me. "You are the writer of the family, I remember."

I was surprised, since I had only gotten to see her 1-2 times a year, but whenever I would see her, I would ask her for stories to transcribe, and I would show her my stories written in beaten up spiral notebooks. Despite not having a high school education, my grandmother would read and read, dreaming of becoming an author and sharing her life with the world.

When she was 80, my dad published her diaries that she had written day by day, from age 14 to 80, documenting her life and the history of our family. Writing is in my blood. I am sure writing kept her sane too, with 6 kids, and countless grandkids.

What is it about writing and painting that keep us sane? What is it about hand to paper or canvas, movement of hands, strokes of ink and paint that feel like healing? How does it help us heal? Will we ever feel better?

With the lack of equitable mental healthcare and resources in this country, we are at a loss. There are many things that are not accessible, and people don't have time to stop and read academic psychology journals or sometimes, be able to afford therapy.

Within my narrative of overcoming one of the most traumatic events of my life through art, I wanted to take the time to go through the academic and psychological routes of the importance of art therapy. To make research accessible and for the chronicle of my narrative through writing and art, I hope this project finds you, and I hope you find healing and wisdom.

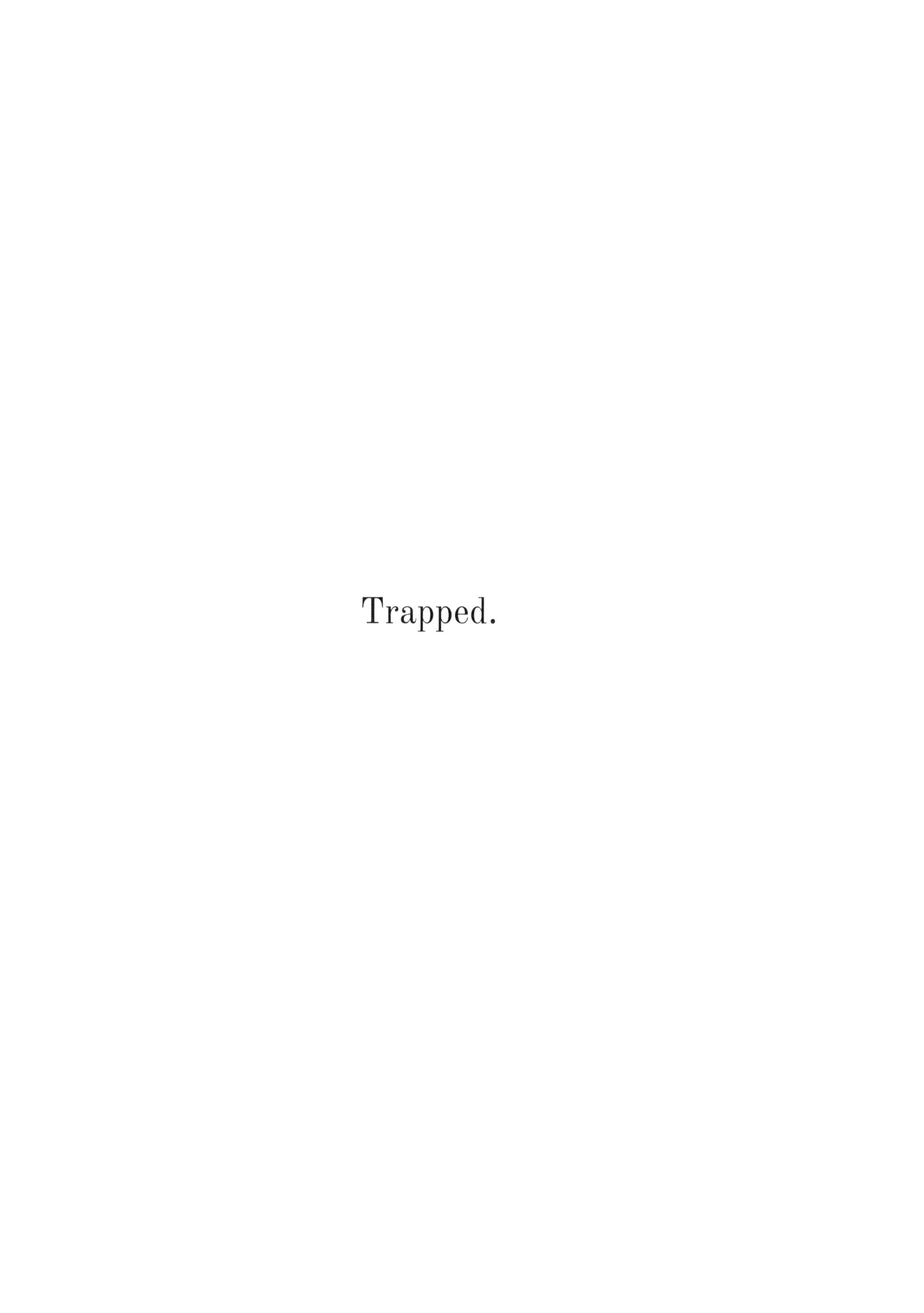

Trapped.

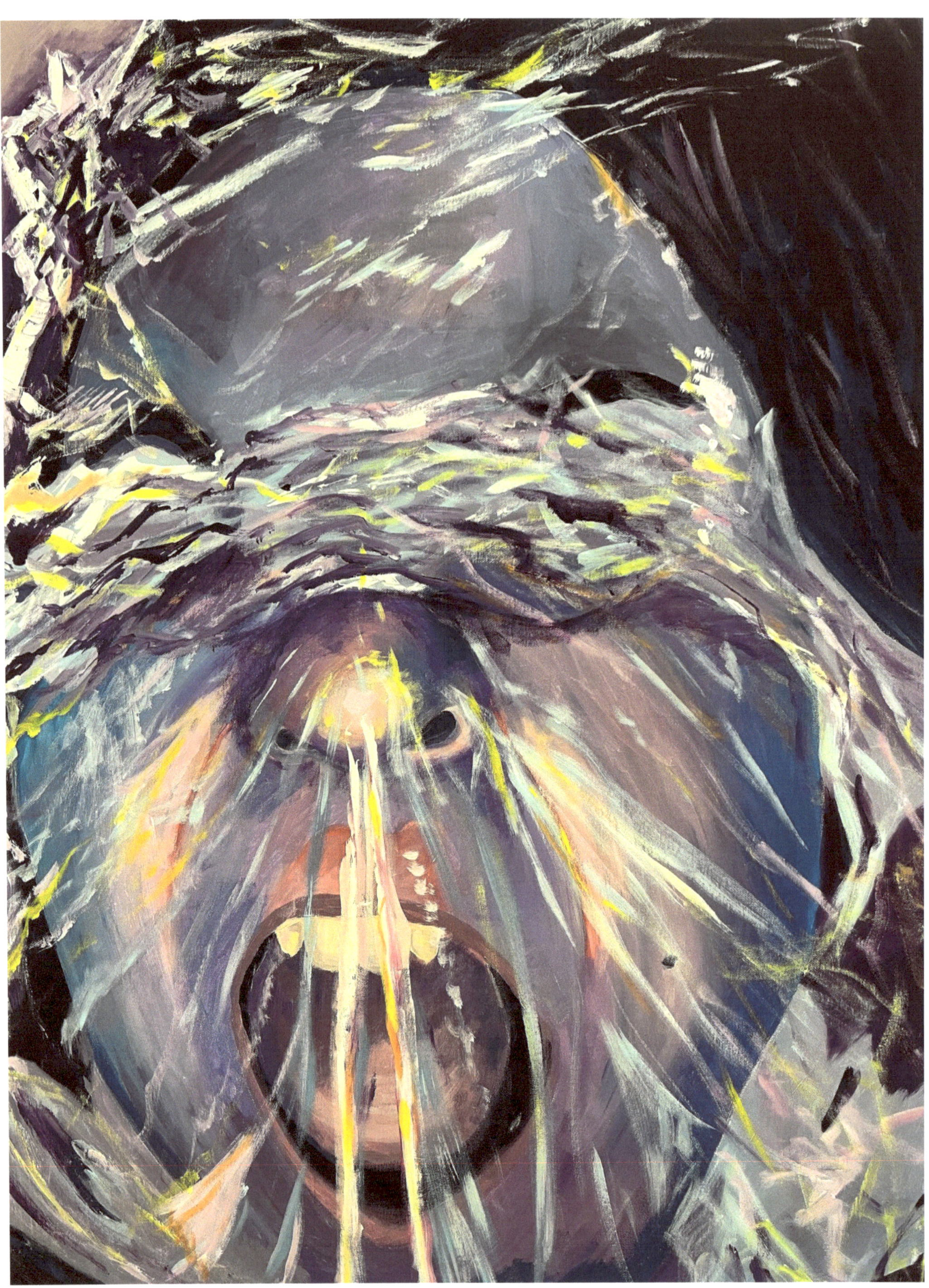

After 2 months, in October, with a promise ring on my finger, and brushing off past transgressions that he had suffered through, I was determined to make it work, despite possible roadblocks. 19 years old with the weight of the future on my shoulders. I wanted to please someone that would give me attention and love. 19 years old and ambitious, studying government, advocacy and policy, I had done everything I could at my university to make it a better place. I had helped lead sexual assault and domestic violence awareness and prevention workshops, working with the university police and advocacy center. Little did I know that I would overlook the very literal signs that I had been trying to teach others.

It was a slow burn, but the bursts of fire scarred deep.

There was one night in October close to Halloween, where I was very busy with midterms. I got a frantic call from my boyfriend who wanted to kill himself. I was worried. I knew he had limited resources, so I went out and prepared a little care package and immediately drove 45 minutes to his house. By the time I got there, he was perfectly fine, with not a care in the world. That was the first time, and the positive reinforcement that would ultimately be my downfall.

Then, there is December.

I picked up my best guy friend to have a nice day at a local small town by the river, about 15 minutes from our houses.

Again, a frantic call from my boyfriend, telling me he will kill himself. If I call the police, he will die by being shot at by the police. At 20 years old, I could have never fathomed such an intense thought, and an immense weight fell upon me to *save* him.

Apologetically, I had to leave my best guy friend by the river. I jumped in my car, driving an hour with traffic, to his house. Sitting in my car in traffic, all I could see in my mind was 3 police cars outside his house, with officers standing in position with the safety off on their guns, pointed at him on the steps of his house. He would be standing there screaming at them at the top of his lungs, pretending that his pellet gun was a shotgun. I could not get there soon enough.

I finally got there, parked, and went into his house.

He grumbled something about me spending time with a guy that was not him, and that men and women could not be friends. After I gave him a hug and reassurance, and after 5 minutes of attention, he was back to 'normal'.

That was one of the many instances, but specifically one of the larger ones that stood out in my mind, because not only did it affect me, but I had abandoned my best friend on that December day. I was abandoning my values, the people I love so much and made me who I am for someone who was so new to my life. That was the beginning of my suspicions, but not enough to shake me from my trance.

Late January, 5 months deep. I was in my own apartment, so alone, 20 years old, feeling miserable. His misery and negativeness dragged me down into a depressive hole, I felt trapped, like I was dry drowning. So I almost broke it off.

However, he promised to make it better.

He would go to therapy, only if I found him one. So, he gave me his insurance information, looked for network therapists, called around, made him an appointment, and he began to go. The weeks he went, he seemed to act better. The weeks he did not go, he was angry and vindictive. Yelling and screaming was never out of the question.

In my sleep, I learned to hold my breath so I would not snore, or else he would lash out. One night, he heard my snoring and went into the basement. I heard him smashing in the walls with a baseball bat, and after that I knew I was not safe to sleep. I could feel the walls shake, and through the vent I heard his angry squawks. If I stayed over, I would not sleep. I would simply close my eyes, and control my breathing patterns.

I felt so trapped. It felt like there was no way out. He would seem to be better some days, but other days were a living hell. I tried to reason with myself that there were always going to be bad days and that no one was perfect. I looked at the promise ring on my finger, cringing at the fact that it could turn into a diamond ring one day. I tried to reason that he could be fixed with therapy. I believed that no one would love me the way he would, despite not having much in common, beside spending time together. Letting him talk about his interests most of the time, and him not caring about the things I did or my accomplishments.

March. 7 months deep.

He started a job, he promised me he was changing. He was working toward supporting us having a life together. The thought of a house with a white fence, a freshly mowed yard, a kid, a dog, and the stability of knowing that everything is in its place, and there is a place for everything in my life sounded like a dream. Going to a Swedish furniture store and picking out the furniture and plants we would have was so much fun, even if the drive there had a terrifying amount of road rage. As much as I tried to rationalize the temporary improvements, nothing would truly change. The true trap was rationality grounded in delusion.

Don’t let the windshield wipers squash you.

Two Times

I yelled "stop!" two times,
two times.
once for the first swerve to the left,
Once for the second swerve to the right.

Two times, I yelled "Stop!" twice.
Once for the first time you said you would
run us off the road.
Once for the time I saw you weren't breaking
fast enough for my comfort.

Red Lights

Everything was hazy,
but I swore I could see the red lights coming.
On the way back,
we hit every red light.
On his way to come get me,
he hit every red light
And with his anger,
I saw every red light.

Blue Fingernails and Nose Blee

My fingernails turn blue from
my lack of iron and my newfound
ability to not retain heat.
My nose bleeds everyday,
from allergies or stress.
In the shower,
I watch sadly and uncontrolably
as my blood drains down
mixed with soap and water
from my nose
like a scene from psycho.
Maybe my body is mad at me
for an all too forgiving heart,
and it deprives the creative hands
of oxygen.
Maybe my heart is punishing
my body for the lack of oxygen
I gave it last Friday night.
Maybe my bloodstream is trying
to bleed out the adrenline
you caused in a fight or flight
where my only options were to
scream or beam.

April. 8 months in.

This month was absolute chaos.

I recorded a Tedx talk on a Tuesday. That Friday night, I was screaming at the top of my lungs to save my life.

He was on my way to pick me up from an acquaintance's apartment, and he called me, yelling and cursing about how bad the traffic was, and how much of an inconvenience it was. I was so embarrassed because I had never hung out with this group outside of my classes. They all looked at me, mortified. I told them not to worry, he usually gets mad like this, and it will blow over quickly.

The core sentence of realization slipped out of my mouth, unconfidently saying "Don't worry. He is not abusive or anything." That is when my gut feeling of knowing I was outright trapped and in danger devastated me. My 2 classmates walked me outside to his car, and he angrily told me to get in, and I could see the worry on their faces. I was in a hazy sequence.

He started driving, and it was about an hour to his house from there. About 30 minutes into the drive, on I-495, he absolutely lost it. He began to scream at the top of his lungs that he was going to kill us, speeding up to 80 miles an hour, swerving between cars recklessly. He said he was done with everything and he will swerve off the road and kill us. The swerving was getting harder and harder. Everything felt like it was going faster and faster.

I have yelled at someone twice in my life, in the entirety of my 22 years. The first time, I was 13 and yelled at my 12 year old cousin over her rude behavior, and then I felt bad and cried.

The second time, I was 20 years old, calmly yelling. I was yelling for my life.

"STOP! ____! YOU CAN'T DO THIS! PLEASE CALM DOWN!"

"I DON'T CARE ANYMORE. WE ARE BOTH GOING TO DIE TOGETHER. NOTHING MATTERS."

"STOP. SERIOUSLY STOP. YOU NEED TO CALM DOWN. CALM DOWN."

They say that right before you die, you see your life flash before your eyes. I did not see my life flash before my eyes. I saw my parents' life, I saw my friends. I saw the news headline saying that a young woman and her boyfriend accidentally crashed into a ditch off I-495. I saw the police knocking on my parent's door, telling them that I was gone. I saw my best friend at my funeral, a closed casket, because they did not recover me from the metal.

I was not afraid, instead it filled me with *rage*. I was so mad at how selfish he could be. I was angry that he would take my life in vain, and no one would know except me, who would be dead. I never feared death, I came to terms with the thought of death at a very young age. Maybe it was growing up in church with the promise of eternal life after death. Maybe it was the acceptance that everything goes black, and everything just stops.

At that moment, I bitterly thought to myself, "No one would know that I am being abused." That night was the worst wake up call that I could have ever gotten. All of those visuals and thoughts rushed through my head in a 3 minute period, while I was yelling for my life.

The car ride after that was awkward. We went to Taco Bell. I was not that hungry. We got back, and he went to sleep. I closed my eyes and controlled my breathing. I did not want a second scare that night. I knew I was unsafe. I was an hour away from my car, I could not leave.

The next morning, we went out to breakfast. He asked me if the night before scared me. Then he specifically asked if it made me feel unsafe. I was stupidly honest, and I told him that I did feel unsafe at that moment. He was angry at me, telling me that if I felt unsafe that it was not good for our relationship. He said I would leave him because of it. I was so scared, I assured him I would not leave him. He was satisfied. I was still an hour away from my car. I could not leave.

We went antique shopping. He finally drove me back, and dropped me off.

I don't remember much from that week. I remember going to the art store and buying a notebook that was on sale that had a bug pattern on it, and the cover said "Don't let the windshield wipers squash you". I bought it. I wrote cryptic writing about that night, along with a recount of the leftover adrenaline that was still rushing through me, even a week later. Throughout this time, I had to act normal with him. I knew that I had to get out. I just did not know how.

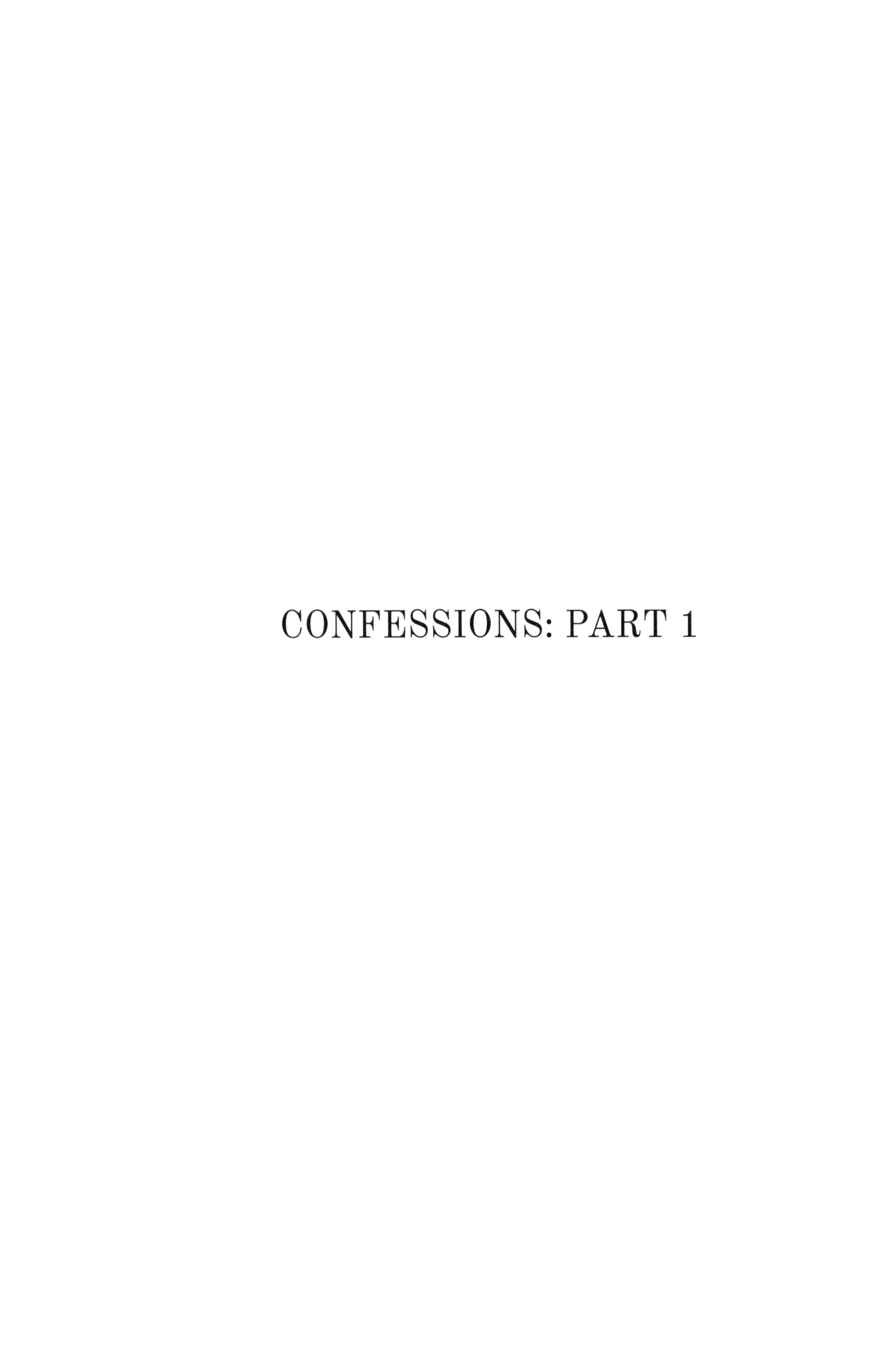

CONFESSIONS: PART 1

CONFESSIONS: PART I

→ I AM NOT WHO I USED TO BE AT ALL. I CANT EVEN IMAGINE GOING BACK. THE THINGS I DID TO LASH BACK AT SOMEONE IN ANGER + RESENTMENT ONLY HURT ME. WHICH, I GUESS IS WHAT THEY WANTED.

→ I DONT KNOW HOW I USED TO LIVE LIKE THAT. TO SEE A GUN HELD UP TO A MAN'S HEAD 1-2x PER WEEK AND TOLD IT'S BECAUSE YOU HAVE FRIENDS OR FAMILY OR SCHOOL IS TERRIFYING.

→ I CANT SAY IM SCARED OF DYING, BUT ANGRY AT THE THOUGHT OF IT. I'VE WORKED TOO DAMN HARD NOT TO LIVE.

April, Continued.

A couple weeks after that rush of adrenaline, there was the gift that keeps on giving. He had applied to buy a certain gun that he wanted, due to his special interests in history. He was denied by the state to buy a gun. That was the tipping point. He went to his mother's house, while she was gone, and pulled the hand gun out of the closet.

I got a video call, so I answered it. My heart dropped. I saw him holding a loaded handgun up to his head, yelling that he would take his life, right there and then. Because he could not buy the gun he wanted. He was banned by the government from possessing a gun. He said if I called the police, he would shoot at them and then die by suicide by cops. I was in a stand still, having to negotiate with rationality grounded in delusion.

I had no other choice but to text his mom. She called him while I was on the video call with him. She talked him down from it. It took both of us.

This was not the first or last time he did this. There was more. When someone uses guns to threaten to hurt themselves because you are trying to maintain other life relationships, or at the drop of a hat with any excuse, they might as well be holding the gun up to you. The feeling of the weight of guilt hangs over your head, that if they take their life, their blood is on your hands. It is absolutely not the case. People have free will.

However, when you are taken hostage, you will never feel the tension ease off you. It was time to plan an escape plan. I booked a flight to Denver, Colorado a couple days after that night. I had to break free.

May.

At the beginning of May, he started taking me to church. We drove an hour to church every Sunday morning from May to June. We would get dressed up in our Sunday clothes, and everything felt weirdly empty. I would just cry to myself during the hymns, praying to God for a way out. I had felt so alienated from God, even though I had grown up in a very Christian environment, with my dad's American family in the bible belt and the cultural staple of church from my mom's Mexican background. I wasn't angry at God, but I just felt abandoned. I wasn't sure if the abandonment was by my own sin, like a karma, or if it was simply just evil in the world. Maybe it was a little of both. I almost felt sick, sitting in those pews before God with the devil sitting next to me, holding my hand.

Mid May, I flew to Denver, CO, my first trip out on my own, funded by my own savings, alone. I knew I needed to learn how to be alone. I knew I needed to gather the strength within myself to leave. I hitched a ride from the airport by chance through mutual friends that lived there. It was my first time meeting them. He was upset that I would meet these 'strangers'. He could not monitor my actions, he could not be on long calls with me. I was at their apartment hanging out. Throughout the trip, I learned so much.

My aunt who I had not seen in 10 years picked me up from my hotel and drove me from Denver to Colorado Springs. She took me to Colorado Springs and I got to hike through Garden of the Gods. I had never felt so alive in that moment of high elevation, with shorter bursts of oxygen. When I finally experienced how much more there was out there in the world, full of so many beautiful sights, I realized that I was capable and worthy of seeing them.

I thought about how a month before, there was the chance that I could never see the way the light hit the mountainous structure, the glowing skies, and the lush fields. I would never have been able to breathe in fresh air. I would never have been able to *breathe*. I got to hang out in Denver with strangers I met on the street, eating meals with them, and walk the botanical gardens by myself on a beautiful spring day. I got messages and calls to try to hook me ino being miserable, but I was not biting. I still felt trapped in the background, but waking up alone did not feel so bad. I was finally starting to understand that being myself, by myself, was not so bad.

June.

My dad got terribly ill. He had a massive heart attack, the emergency room team spent an hour reviving him. He was legally dead at one point, but they never gave up on him. He came back, woke up long enough for me to say I loved him, and he went into a week long coma. My dad woke up on Father's Day, affirming that he was going to make it.

My boyfriend drove me to the hospital to see my dad when he coded. He sat with me and comforted me. I was grateful to not be alone, and I almost, for a second, thought that maybe everything was fine. I realized one thing: this situation, as horrible as it was, presented an opportunity to get out. So, I broke up with him late June. He brought me gifts, showered me in loving words, convincing me things would be better. A large gift bags of my favorite snacks, candies, and some flowers I liked. I was appalled by the small act of kindness.

However, I did not feel brave enough to get out yet, so I took him back.

He knew.

GOD,

FORGIVE THEM,

BECAUSE HE KNEW

~~FOR THEY DON'T KNOW WHAT THEY'VE DONE~~

HE KNEW.

July.

I knew that I needed to get out for sure. Despite driving 2 hours to the hospital to see my dad, spending 12+ hours a day there, for about a month at this point, he was somehow draining more energy from me than I could imagine. The selfishness never stopped. It was a lot of back and forth, talking about issues that did not relate to me or my situation, a continual tax on my mind. I had to not only hold my family up, but keep him entertained and out of bad mind sets. I did not have time to devote to talking to him as much as I did before, which was all day, every day and every night.

So, I cut it off for good. For 6 days after the break up, I received harassing texts and messages, with extreme content. He sent me pictures of his speedometer at 120mph, saying he was recklessly driving because he could not live without me, and it would be my fault. He sent me a video link to a man committing suicide. That one was the worst for me to see, with a background of having intense bipolar with psychotic tendencies. I saw that video in my mind for months after.

I had enough. I texted his mom a 4 paragraph text, detailing everything he had done, at 6:30 a.m. At 8 a.m., I got a text from him cursing me out for "worrying his mom with fake sh*t". Fake sh*t, you say? Well, that was the breath of confidence I had to completely block him on every possible thing I had. If it was fake, I knew that the blood was not on my hands. I could wipe my hands clean and be done. It was all fake. I felt so free knowing that he knew what he had done.

CONFESSIONS: PART 2

CONFESSIONS PART II

→ I AM BLUNT AND HONEST AND OPEN BUT THERE IS SO MUCH I DONT SAY. THE EXTENT OF DANGER + FEAR IVE EXPERIENCED WILL NEVER COME OUT. I HATE PITY. I'M SICK OF IT. I HATE THE SAD EYES AND PITY HUGS. I DON'T CARE. MOST PEOPLE DONT EITHER. IT'S JUST LIFE. I DONT WANT PITY, I WANT RESPECT.

→ I DONT KNOW WHAT FEAR IS ANYMORE AND MAYBE, THAT KINDA SCARES ME.

→ I WILL NEVER FEEL ACCOMPLISHED. I NEVER HAVE FELT IT. I JUST DO THINGS. I THINK ITS BECAUSE THE PEOPLE I LOVE DON'T SEE THEM.. OR CARE.

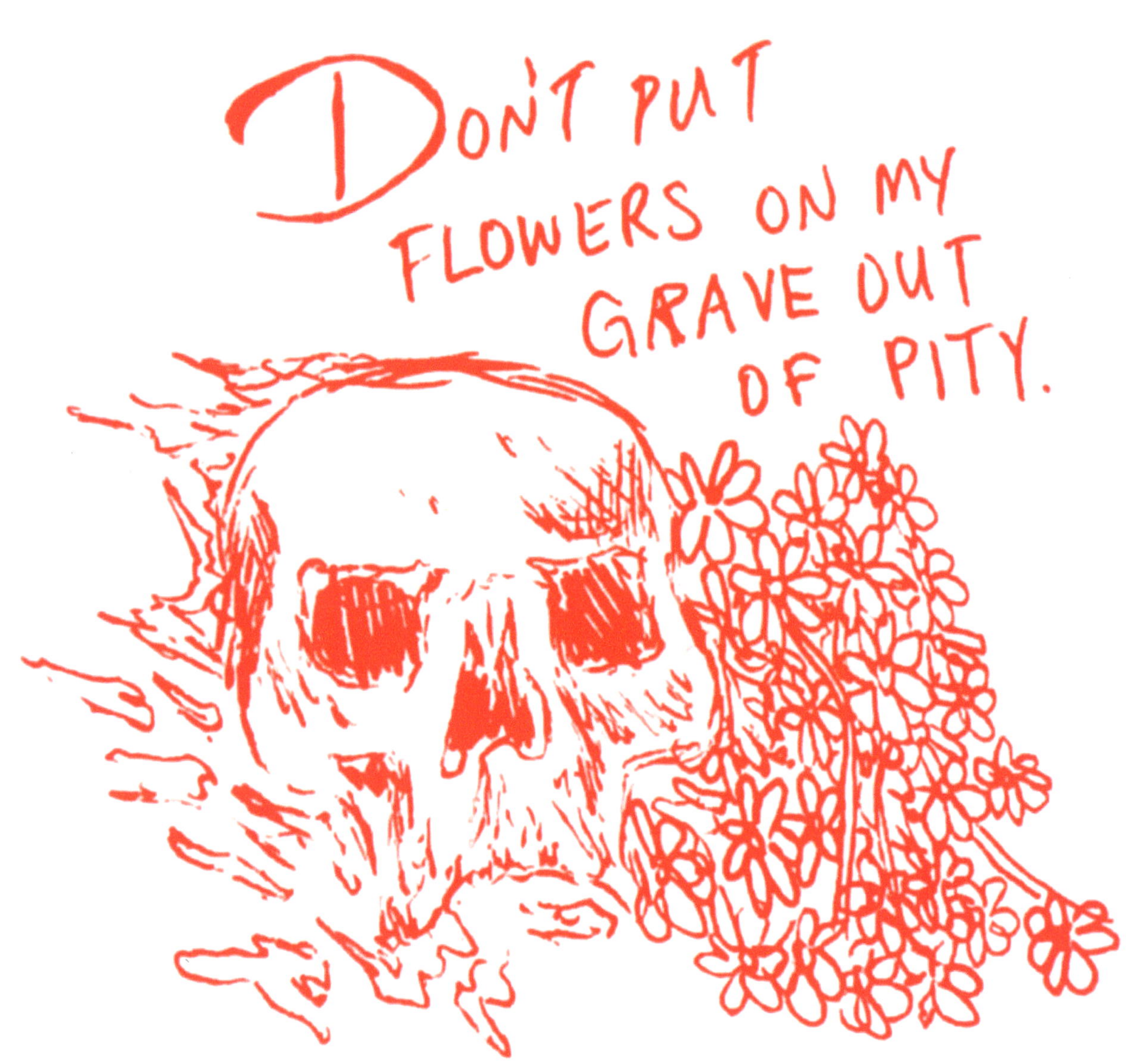
DON'T PUT
FLOWERS ON MY
GRAVE OUT
OF PITY.

Post July.

I pushed everything down from mid July in my newfound freedom, to Mid August. I had to train on how to be a Residential Assistant for my dorm building, and we had to do exercises on emergency activities during the week of training. They had school counselors stationed outside, and I had to run out of the training because I felt a wave of nausea and terror. The counselor stood there with me, and let me talk about how the attempt against my life and the immense fear I felt. I will never forget what she said to me.

"That.... Really sucks. Sorry."

I was in shock. I could not stomach the pity, nor could I handle the fact that in that moment, I felt like no one truly cared. I wanted to push it down even more. I did not want to tell anyone what happened. It was like being hostage again. As blunt and open as I am, I felt as if I could not speak without being pitied. I hate pity. I hate people looking at me with sad eyes, I hate the pats on the back, I hate the way they brush me off as a traumatized child. **Pity is simply an empty expression to fill the void of being speechless. Pity is not empathy, pity is the simplification of not caring.**

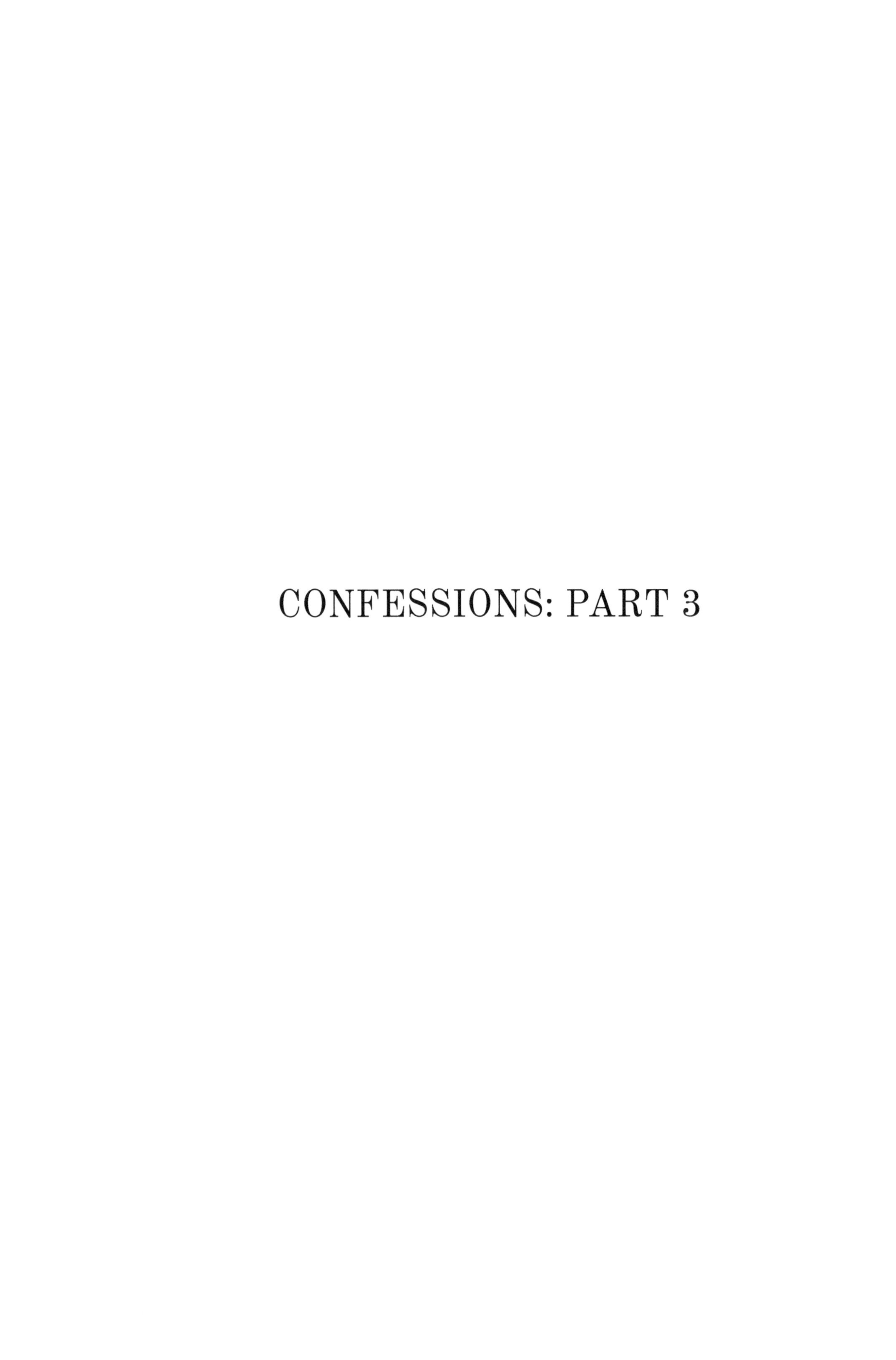

CONFESSIONS: PART 3

CONFESSIONS PART III

→ EVERYTHING EXCEPT LOVE FEELS MEANINGFULLY MEANINGLESS.

→ I DONT THINK I AM AN IMPOSTER, I THINK I JUST GET TOO LUCKY SOMETIMES. I KNOW I AM NOT THE BEST, JUST ME. I WISH I COULD BE GREAT.

→ I AM 21 AND HARDLY ACCEPT THE FACT THAT I AM AN ADULT. THIS WAS EVERYTHING I THOUGHT I WANTED. ITS SOMETHING...

→ I MAY BE DESCRIBED AS A FORTRESS OR A SANDCASTLE OR A LANDFILL BUT I THINK IM JUST A HOUSE OF CARDS. TAKE A GAMBLE, RIGHT?

September to December.

I had stopped making art the way I had used to, which is creating pieces reflecting on how I felt. I still drew everyday, but while I was in the relationship I felt as if I could not make the pieces on how I felt, because they were dark reflections I did not want to face. It needed to start again, since I was free. I had to let it out. So I began to draw more, and write.

School was the distraction I thought I needed to cope with everything feeling like it was crashing down around me. It was not. I did not sleep at all. I could only take naps on my dorm apartment couch, I could not sleep in my own bed, because I felt unsafe. I had somehow fallen into a new relationship with one of my close friends, (I'll call him 'PJ'), and he lived two floors above me. I felt safe sleeping on his couch in his dorm living room some nights. All my other friends were PJ's roommates.

I only attended a couple of my art classes, as I decided early that semester to change my major to a Bachelor of Fine Arts with a minor in Psychology, from studying Government and International Politics with a concentration in policy. I wanted to do art therapy, because I knew art was the only thing keeping me sane. I knew that in the state I was in, I just needed to graduate and get the piece of paper saying I attended a university. My dad's dream has been for me to graduate, since he sacrificed so much to get me through.

Classes were nearly impossible though. I could not go to class without sitting there for half an hour, propelled into spiraling panic attacks, obsessively checking my phone for the time and to see if my family would text and perhaps say they were in danger, since he knows where I lived. I would be sitting in class, and my professor would fade away from my sight, and instead violent visions of murder and tragedy would flash before my eyes. I had never experienced psychotic visions before then. I had been off my bipolar medication for months since they did not seem to work anyway. I was unmedicated, extremely traumatized, not in therapy, and spiraling.

In early October, I was so stressed about school and everything piling up. I decided that it would be best to take a Saturday excursion to Philadelphia, because I wanted to see the art museum there.

The Philadelphia Art Museum was the first art museum I had ever gone to. My dad took me there when I was 15, a freshman in high school. He wanted to make my first trip to an art museum special, since I had loved art so much. That first trip changed the trajectory of my life and how I viewed art.

The first painting that moved my soul was a Van Gogh painting. It is called "Rain". It is a dreary blue, gray, and green painting that depicts rain in the wheatfields of France, that Van Gogh observed from outside his window from the hospital he was in. It was made the same year he died.

I didn't know that art had the impact to move people up until that point. Standing in front of that painting made me realize two things: First, Emotion is very real in art, and second, How do I do that? Even though my dad had taken me there to see Van Gogh's sunflowers, the Rain washed that all away. After that trip, my art transformed into an emotional outlet, rather than an aesthetic outlet.

Going there at 20, 5 years later, with a lot of life experience under my belt was just what I needed to get a little bit of fresh air. I walked around the museum, enjoyed the sights, touristed around Philly a bit, and drove home. I went with PJ, and it was a fun day. As soon as I drove us back from Philly, parked, and had my foot hit the pavement of the parking lot, I felt like I was drowning underwater.

I immediately announced that I needed to go to the emergency room. PJ begged me not to drive, and that he would drive me. I have not let people drive me since the incident, however, so I took my keys, and drove myself 45 minutes to the hospital. The next thing I know, I am being woken up by a nurse. "Please, stay awake. You need to stay awake!" "Why can't I take a nap? I am so tired and feel sick." "If you go to sleep, you will die."

Having a nurse look like she is going to cry, while telling you that staying awake was a matter of life and death, and giving you oxygen prongs for your nose is a way to wake up. After a 14 hour day at this point, driving 5 hours all by myself, being a Philly tourist, and driving to the hospital was absolutely nothing to me, compared to the events my ex boyfriend put me through. I was not scared to die. I was amused. After everything I had gone through to survive, here I am on my deathbed, 4 months after escaping, 6 months after the attempt on my life.

I was hospitalized and put into the intensive care unit for a week. My lung partially collapsed and I had bronchitis. At one point, I was almost awakened by a zap to the chest from the emergency response team, but the nurse shook me hard enough to wake me up that time. My oxygen had dropped to 68. After a week, I was able to go home. However, one thing I did while I was not sleeping was draw. I had my sketchbook and full marker set with me. It felt good to draw, after being inspired by the art museum.

On my 21st birthday, a stormy evening in late October, I was taking a nap on the couch while PJ sat with me, and he woke me up. I had kept mumbling apologies in a scared tone about me sleeping. “I am so sorry I am snoring.... I am so sorry... I didn’t mean to make noise... I didn’t mean to..” PJ was concerned, but then we started getting ready for my birthday dinner.

Right before we went out, I went to the bathroom and it hit me why I was so afraid. I could see my ex boyfriend screaming, waving around a baseball bat. I could feel my chest tighten, I could remember the nights I closed my eyes for survival, I realized that my body had adapted to waking up and being on guard, constantly monitoring my breathing. The worst realization was knowing the war was over, but your body will keep fighting. The way your physical body can still be fighting, even though you are safe.

It was my birthday though, so I put on a red cowboy hat and went to Texas Roadhouse with PJ and a couple friends. I made it through with a couple drinks, dancing in the parking lot after. It was time for me to move on. It was time to forget. However, it echoed in the back of my mind.

IF MY BODY IS AT WAR WITH ITSELF,

THEN MY BRAIN IS THE POLITICIAN

I HATE SILENCE.

BUT I RESENT MUSIC BECAUSE PEOPLE ACTUALLY LISTEN TO IT.

I RESENT WRITING BECAUSE NOBODY READS IT.

I HATE SPACES I CALL MY OWN BECAUSE I CAN NEVER GET COMFORTABLE OR FEEL SAFE. MAYBE BECAUSE MY BODY IS MY OWN AND ITS NEVER BEEN SAFE, NOR MY MIND.

I CAN NEVER FEEL COMFORTABLE, IT IS ALWAYS HOT OR COLD.

IF MY BODY IS AT WAR WITH ITSELF, THEN MY BRAIN IS THE POLITICIAN.

I DON'T KNOW WHY SOME
NIGHTS I EXPECT TO CLOSE
MY EYES. I AM SIMULTANEOUSLY
THE GREATEST POLITICIAN AND THIEF
PRISONER OF WAR. I AM EXHAUSTION
AND ADRENALINE. MANIC AND EMPTY.
THE LOUD VOICE AND SMALL PRESENCE.
CONFIDENT AND AFRAID. COUNTER
CULTURE BUT ROOTED DEEP INTO
TRADITION. HATER OF BUREARUCRACY
BUT FUNCTIONS BY SYSTEMIC CHAOS.
JUDMENTALLY OPEN MINDED. THE
MOST SINFUL LAMB.

I spent every day with PJ and our friend group, always surrounded by them, until I had to go back to my room at night. Sitting in my dorm room from 11PM-9AM felt so long, like a prison sentence. I did not know how to be alone. I listened to music, I had a lot of snacks, and I played fetch with my cat. The stuff in my dorm room piled up around me until I was drowning in piles of clothes and trash.

I did not invite anyone over because I was too embarrassed about the state of my room; everything fell out of control. I had a couple friends occasionally help dig me out and clean my room sometimes, but asking for help as a 21 year old felt so embarrassing, especially because it was the bare minimum of tasks. The only reason I got out of my room, took a shower, and ate was to see PJ and our friends.

I did not know how to function. My medicine bottles piled up in my drawer, because my mom picked them up and gave them to me, hoping that I was taking it. I was not. My grades were tanking at a steady decline, because I just could not sit in a classroom with people. I did not feel safe. I did not know how to ask anyone for help. All I had was my legal pad to write on, sketching a little in various notebooks, and listening to 70's rock.

My car, ironically, was one of the only places I felt safe. Still is. You would think that near death by car would ruin the peace, but I always loved MY car. My car is where I have control. My hands are on the steering wheel, my foot controls the gas and brakes, I put on my monthly playlists and I am in control. I would not get in anyone's car after the incident.

To this day, I've only gotten in about 5 people's cars in years, and I trust these people with my life. 5 may sound like a large number, but when you're a college student, you need to hitch a ride in a lot of various vehicles. One of the things that kept me sane was going on drives at night, especially late night drives so I could pick up my groceries and essential items. My car was the only thing I got to control.

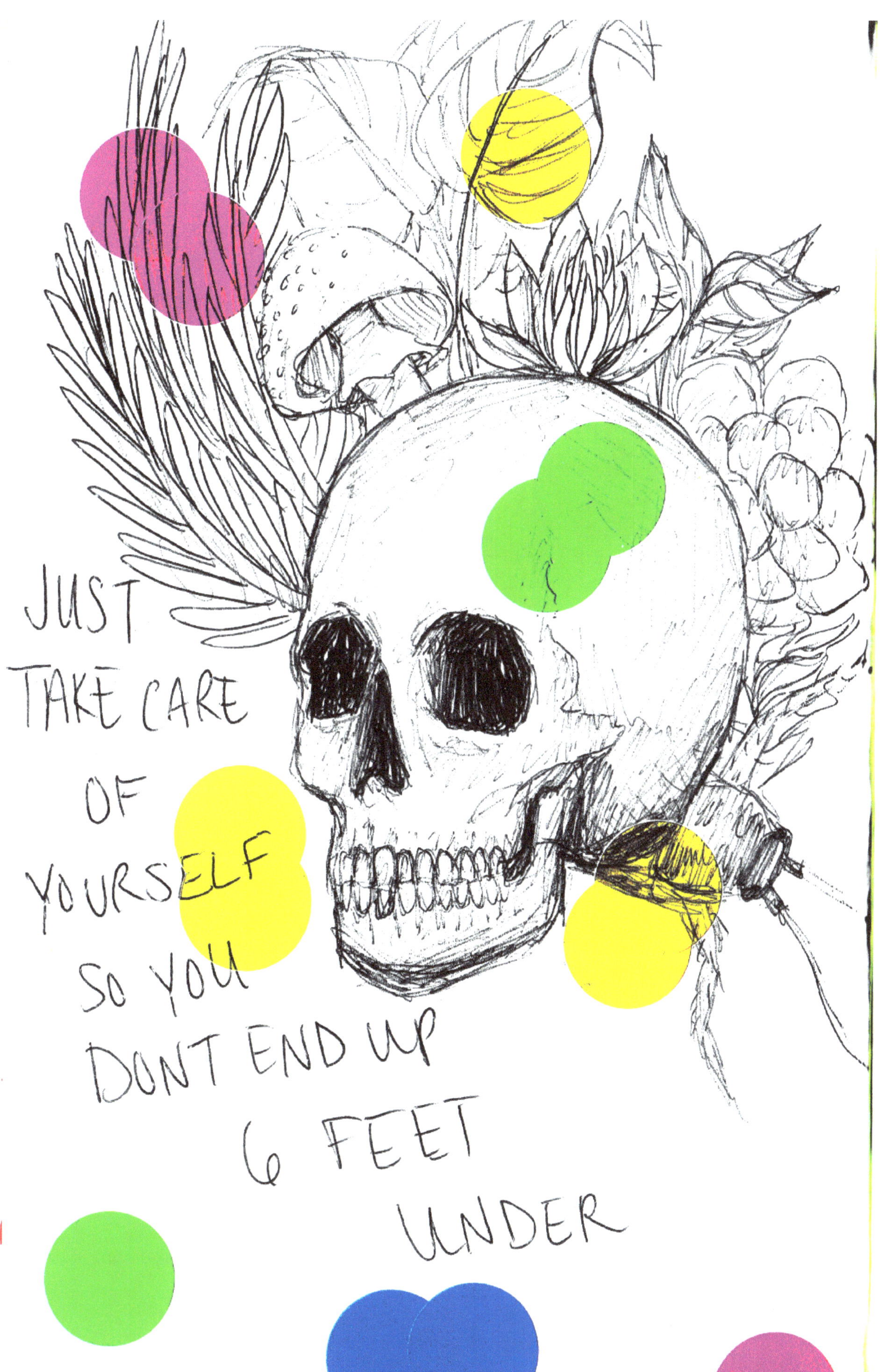
JUST
TAKE CARE
OF
YOURSELF
SO YOU
DONT END UP
6 FEET
UNDER

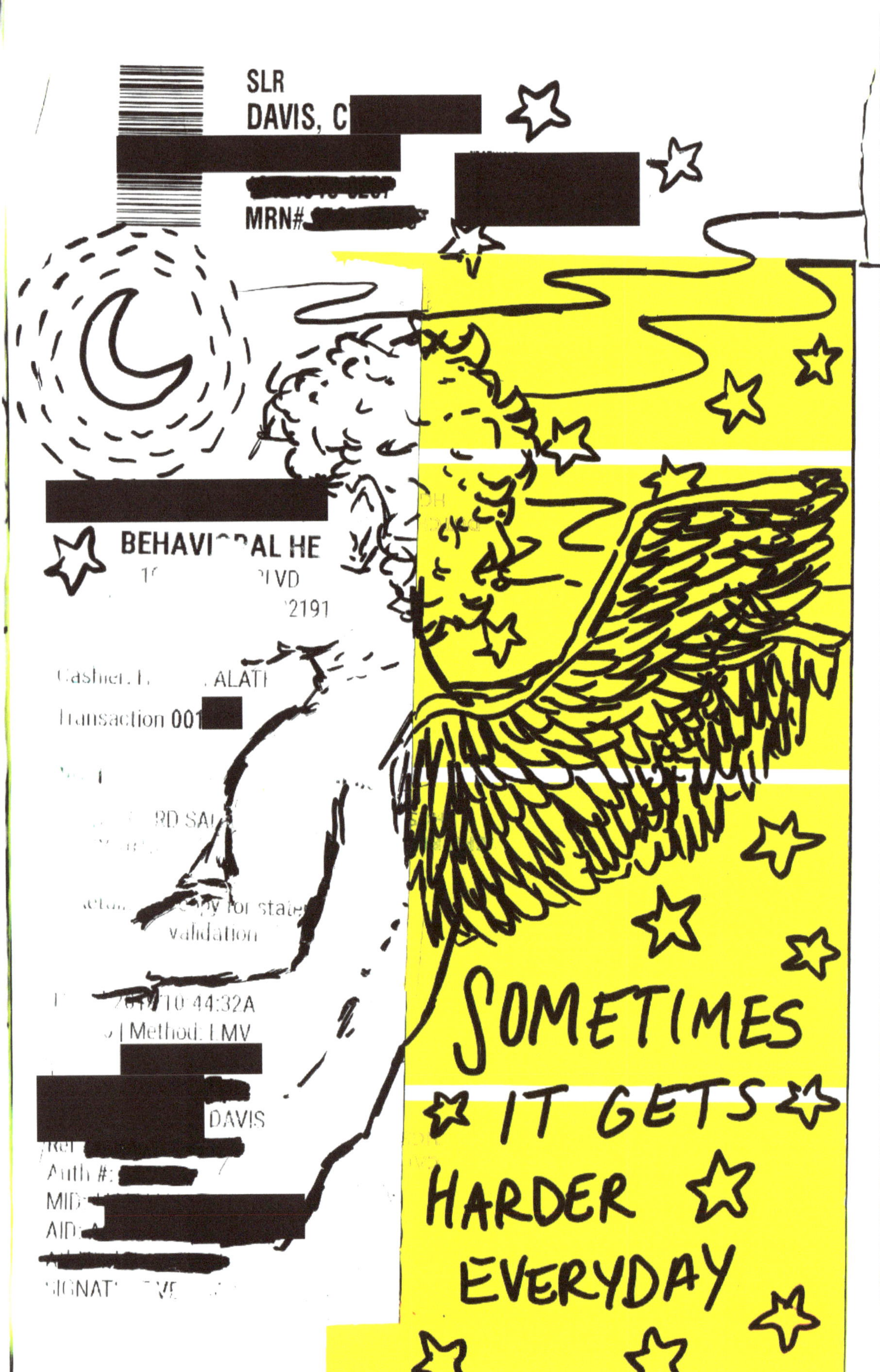
SLR
DAVIS, C
MRN#
BEHAVI AL HE
Cashier:
ALATI
Transaction 001
validation
DAVIS
Auth #:
MID:
AID:
SOMETIMES
IT GETS
HARDER
EVERYDAY

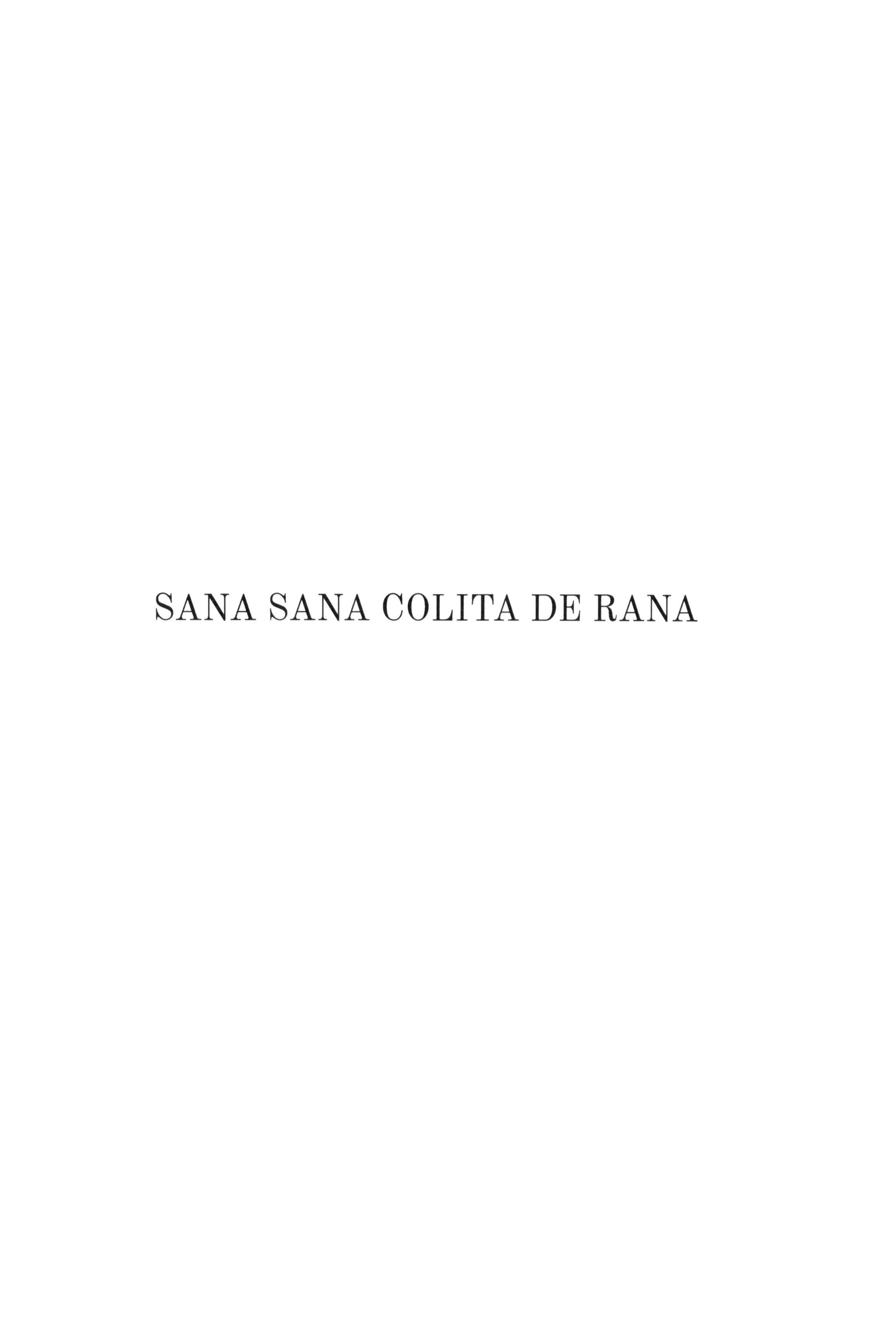

SANA SANA COLITA DE RANA

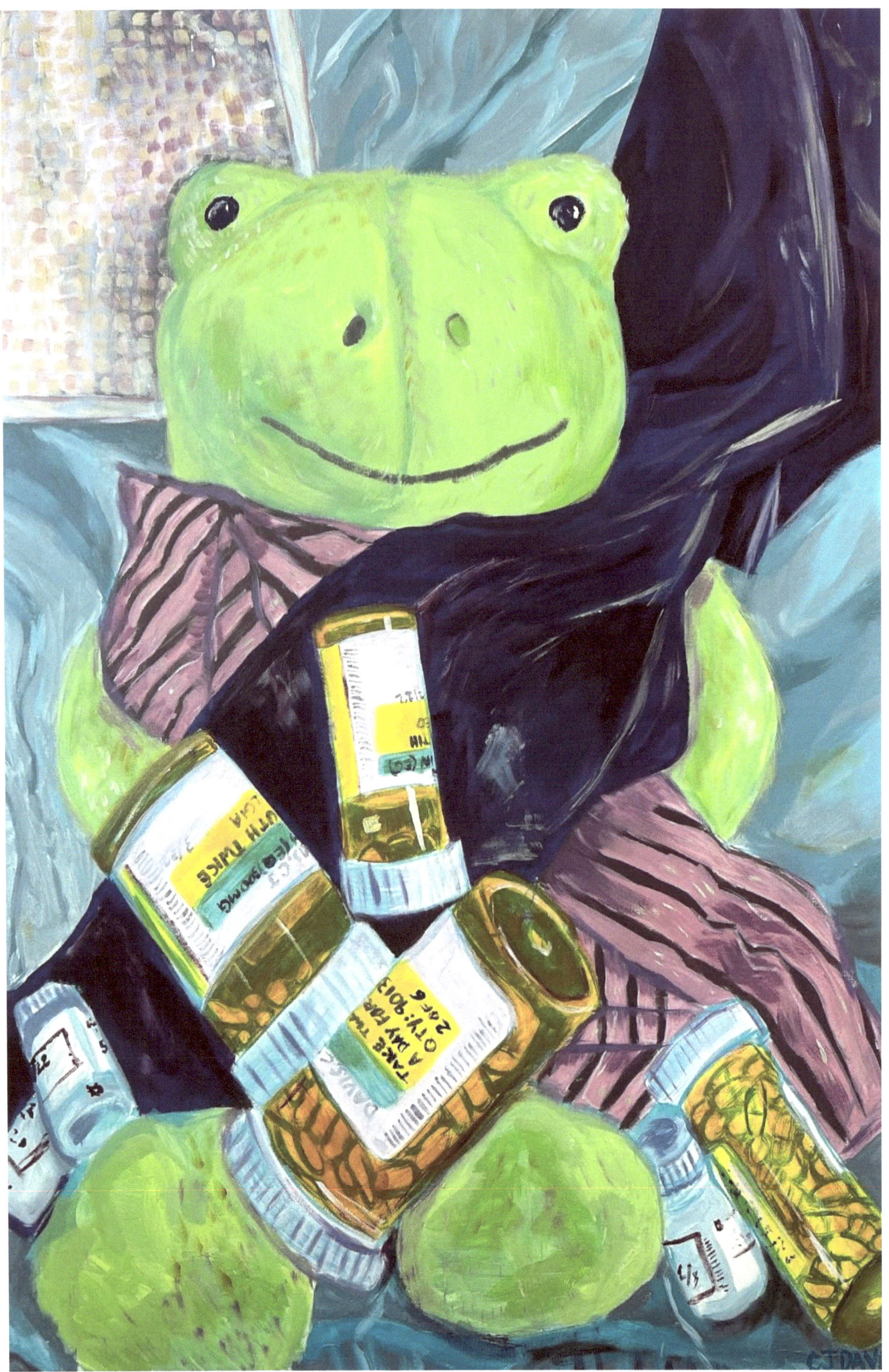

Spring, a year after the attempt on my life.

As the holidays passed and the university winter break came to a close, the spring semester was starting. Since I had changed my major back to fine arts from government and international politics, I needed to start taking art classes again. My previous painting teachers honestly discouraged me from picking up a paint brush again. However, with the encouragement of PJ and my friends, I nervously went to my painting class.

PJ was kind enough to make me a new playlist every week to listen to while I painted. The assignments encouraged me to take my own direction, and I began to feel overwhelming joy that I was there.

March.

Sana, Sana, Colita de Rana is a saying in Latin American culture, which means "heal, heal, little froggie butt," I had the idea to paint my stuffed animal frog, which was the last gift my dad got me before he fell ill, with medicine bottles to symbolize the healing journey my father and I were both on. I was so passionate and proud of that painting, and while it is not the best one I've done, it still holds a place in my heart.

April.

I was the Internal Vice President of organization on campus during this time, Undocu@Mason. The organization has a 10+ year history of advocating for undocumented students and the undocumented community. It is a cause that I feel strongly about, as my mother's family immigrated here from Mexico. I was thrilled that I could be part of such an amazing advocacy group.

A couple other leaders in Undocu@Mason and I put together a pop up art show in 3 months, and while it was only 2 or 3 hours long, we had over 200 people attend. I displayed *Sana, Sana, Colita de Rana*, as well as a portrait painting of my abuela, Estella. One of the professors at the university, a Smithsonian curator, gave me high compliments about my work. I was bursting with excitement and awe. It was a confirmation to me that I was on the right path.

To be on the right path, I knew I had to take myself more seriously, and that meant attending to my health. I booked an appointment with a new psychiatrist and went to the appointment. She had pointed out that my medications I was prescribed were not working because they had canceled each other out. She gave me new medication and I finally began taking medication again. It helped so much.

The one year anniversary of the attempt on my life had arrived. This year, however, I had a sorority formal to attend. I felt awful. As much as I tried to hide it, I ended up leaving early with PJ. When I was back at my dorm, I changed clothes, and I decided to go for a drive. I drove to Taco Bell. This time, I was in control of the drive there. This time, I did not yell for my life. This time, I was safe. I was proud of myself for getting in my car to drive, even if I did not necessarily feel like it. I took control back. I felt like I was healing.

May.

Anxiously pacing after throwing up that morning, it was time for my second Tedx talk. This time, it was in front of a live audience. This talk was about lack of access to mental healthcare in marginalized communities, and sharing my story. Some people may call me crazy to get up in front of a live audience, with cameras recording me with the potential for anyone in the world to watch me for years after, and openly admit that I have Bipolar 2 and PTSD.

I was told so many times that I shouldn't tell people that, how it will affect my opportunity for employment, how I will be ostracized. It made me want to yell it from the rooftops even more. To share that I had PTSD made me feel like I had the control of my own narrative, my own life.

I had met one of my future painting professors there. Little did I know he would become one of the most impactful educators and mentors that I will ever have and had. He encouraged me to take his class that upcoming fall. I think I had shocked him, to get up there and talk about my issues so openly. Or, maybe, it was the fact I brought up art. Perhaps I'll ask him, after he reads this.

Summer came and went, and then fall crept in. A lot of changes happen, like getting out of a relationship, making new friends, seeing old ones, watching people fall apart and heal.

From that August to December, over a year after getting "out," I struggled immensely with personal issues from current relationships I was in around me. It was the first semester back fully in the art program. Psychosis crept in more and more, and the flashbacks got stronger and stronger. I had one thing to ground me, which is painting.

I not only found confidence in my own voice again through painting, but comfort, which was something that I missed. To be able to trust myself again, after I felt like I have made the worst decisions in my life, is an unfathomable level of forgiveness. What truly earned this trust and confidence back, was my first critique with the professor I had met in the spring: Chawky.

My first acrylic series I did in his class was not by any means good work, it had a long way to go. However, he talked about how my openness about my pain empowers others and myself. Empowerment. That was something I wanted to strive for as an advocate, but did not know where to start. It all started with honesty and a paintbrush.

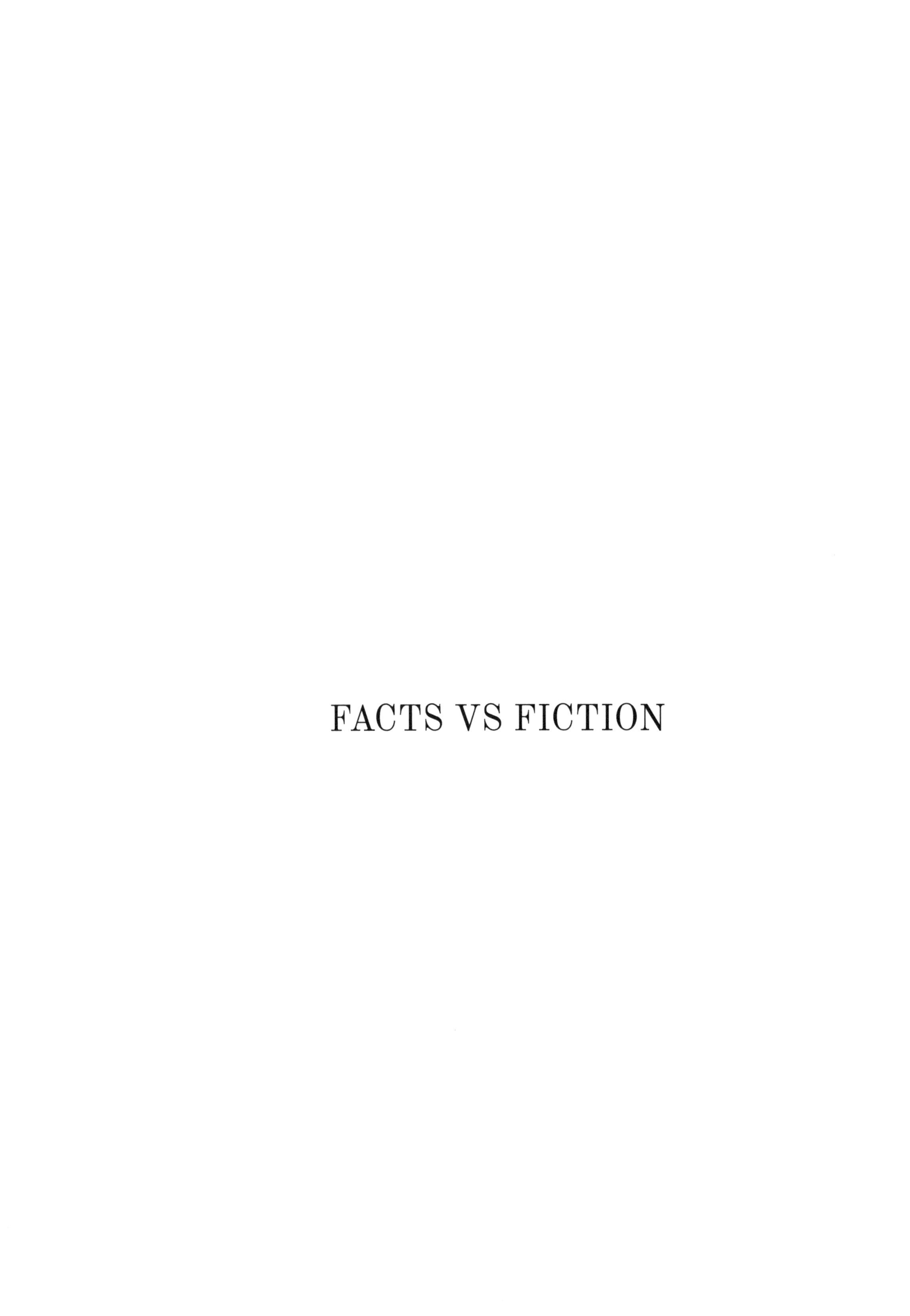

FACTS VS FICTION

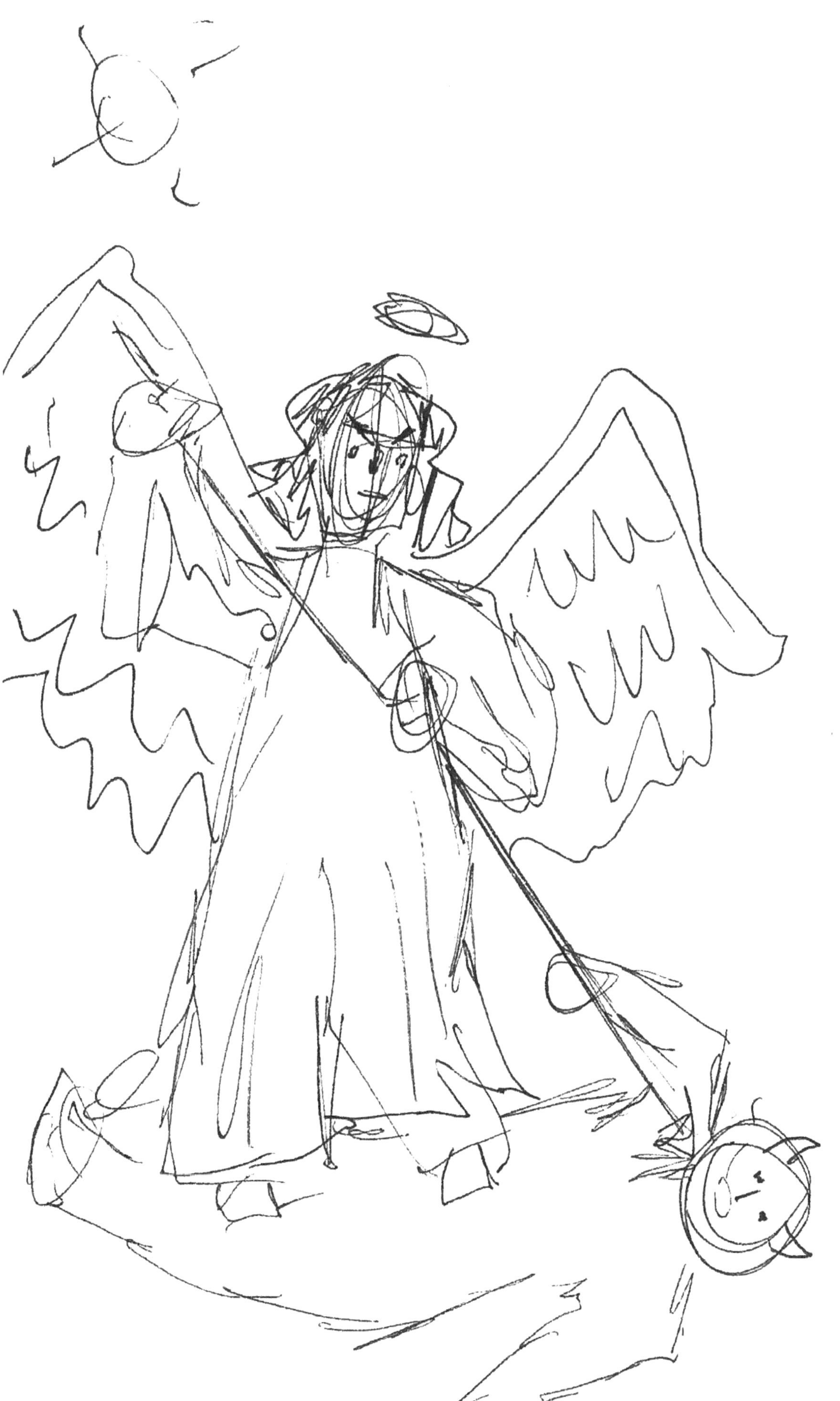

AUG 14 2022

FICTION

I found that I can't take fiction anymore. At the bookstore, I only buy non-fiction. There's so many real issues I can't be ignoring, that feeling for fictional stories takes too much energy. I can't watch Hallmark movies because it stings that love isn't the picture perfect story as it plays out. Fiction stings my soul in a way I can't face. I'd rather have something real so when I feel, I know it's real. Maybe I've been through so much abuse or imbalanced chemicals, that fiction was too real to me. To believe in an illusion for so long, to write a picture perfect story of how things could play out if I could just get through the yelling, the smashing, the anger. If I could just get through this sexual assault, if I could just bear these crosses, then my fairytale would play out. It made me sick to think of those fairytale endings with such evil going on. Fiction, is too real - an illusion that keep our hearts going. Fiction is to believe that everything is black and white, the bad guys being so obvious, the prince charmings being charismatic and loving. No one seems to realize that the prince charmings are charming for thier own self gain. The hero wants glory and power. The bad guys do bad things for thier versions of the right reasons. The princess is in distress because someone put her there in that position. For a me, I put myself in distress because I believed prince charming. Fiction stings because I feel like I will never get my fairytale ending. It makes me sick that I believed in illusions for so long. Life is hard. Love takes work. Lust comes easy, so does pride. We can work, and work away, but life will never be perfect. However, where do we accept the imperfections and still be happy?

"If it were me, I would have just broken up with him after the first bad thing."

"You really put yourself in that situation, you are the only one to blame."

"It really is not that bad, just get over it."

Many underestimate the aftermath pain of trauma, but even more people underestimate the intense apathy that you are targeted with as a survivor of trauma. It is sickening. It makes fiction seem like it mocks your reality, as it feels like it creates false narratives that lead to damaging stigmas.

In an article by Nicole M. Overstreet and Diane M. Quinn in Basic and Applied Social Psychology, they found that "anticipated stigma, internalized stigma, and cultural stigma were prominent barriers to help-seeking from formal and informal support networks." Anticipated stigmas are the fears and stigmas about what will happen once people know about the situation. Internalized stigmas are the stigmas that one believes about themselves, knowing the negative stereotypes surrounding abuse survivors. Cultural stigmas are the general societal stigmas that berate and attempt to discredit survivors of abuse.

Nicole M. Overstreet and Diane M. Quinn's Intimate Partner Violence (IPV) Stigmatization Model is based on these 3 categories of stigma. Although this model is currently a conceptual framework and there is more research to be done, I personally believe through my experience with other survivors and myself, that these three categories of stigmas are the driving factors against getting support. These stigmas are very real, and while stigmas about mental health are currently beginning to change, we need to begin unraveling the stigmas around domestic and intimate partner violence. Start the conversation.

It is not easy to put yourself into the shoes of a survivor of abuse, as knowing what humanity can do is endless, but simultaneously unbelievable. However you feel in the aftermath is acceptable and valid. You are not alone, and there is a community of survivors that have been through similar journeys.

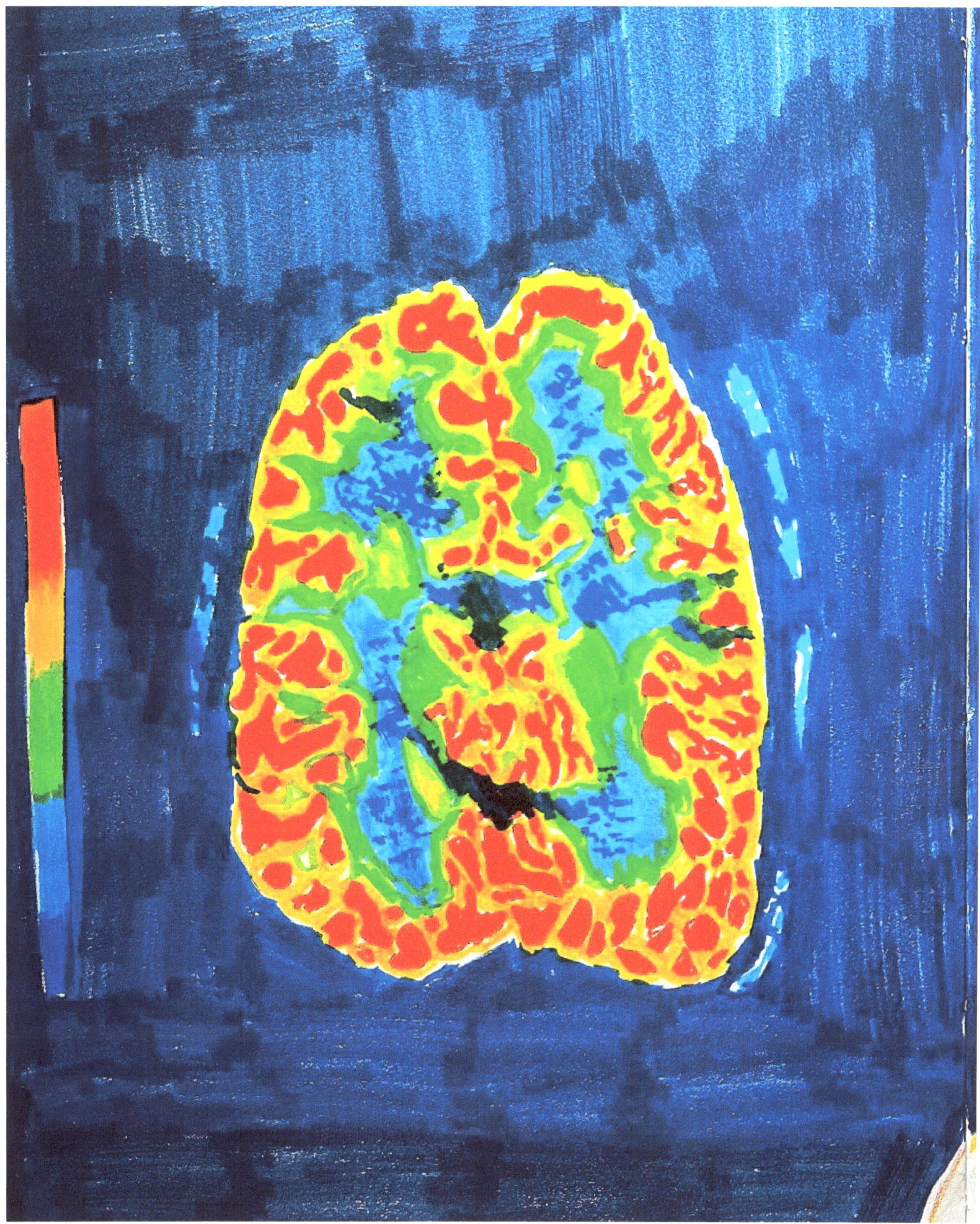

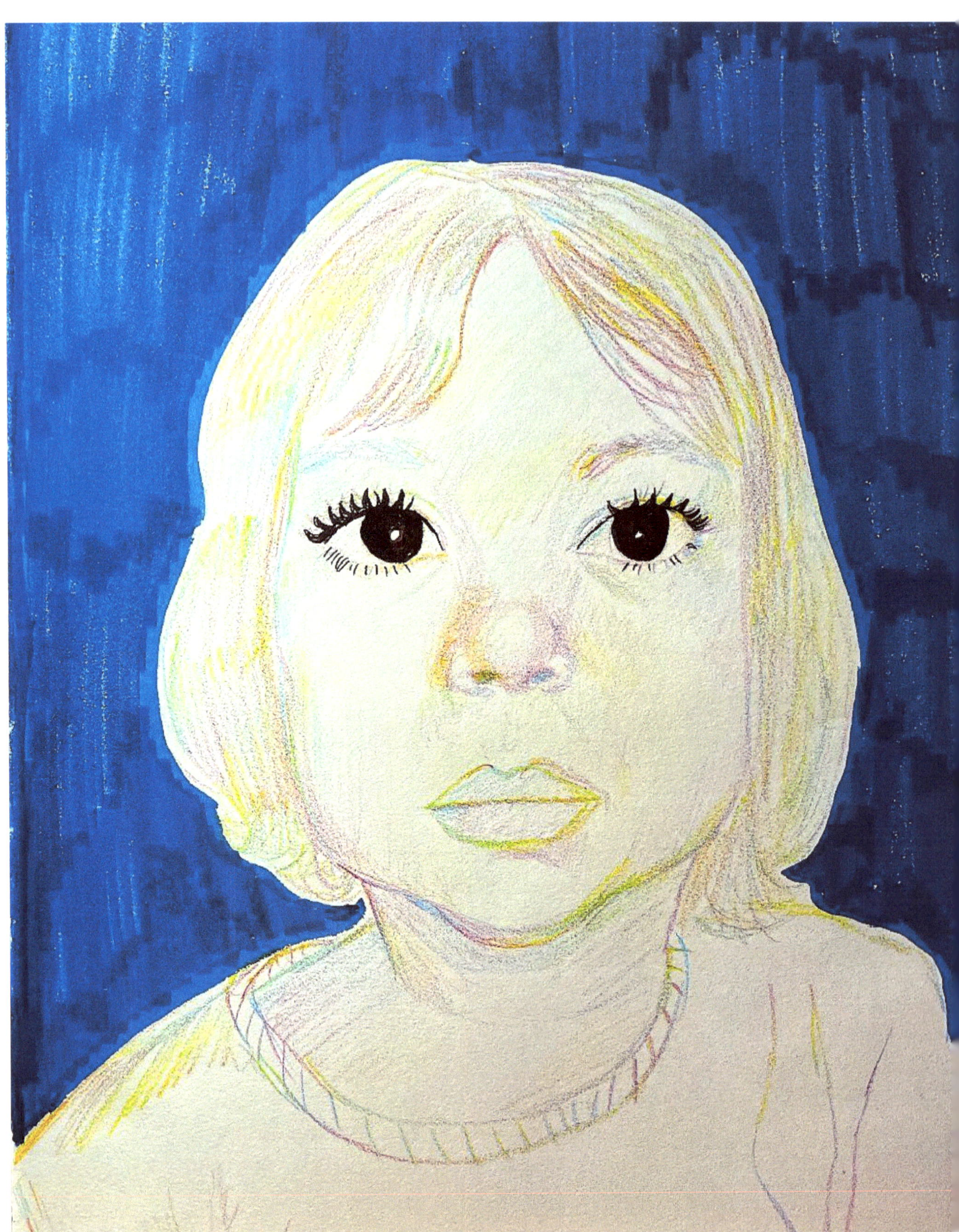

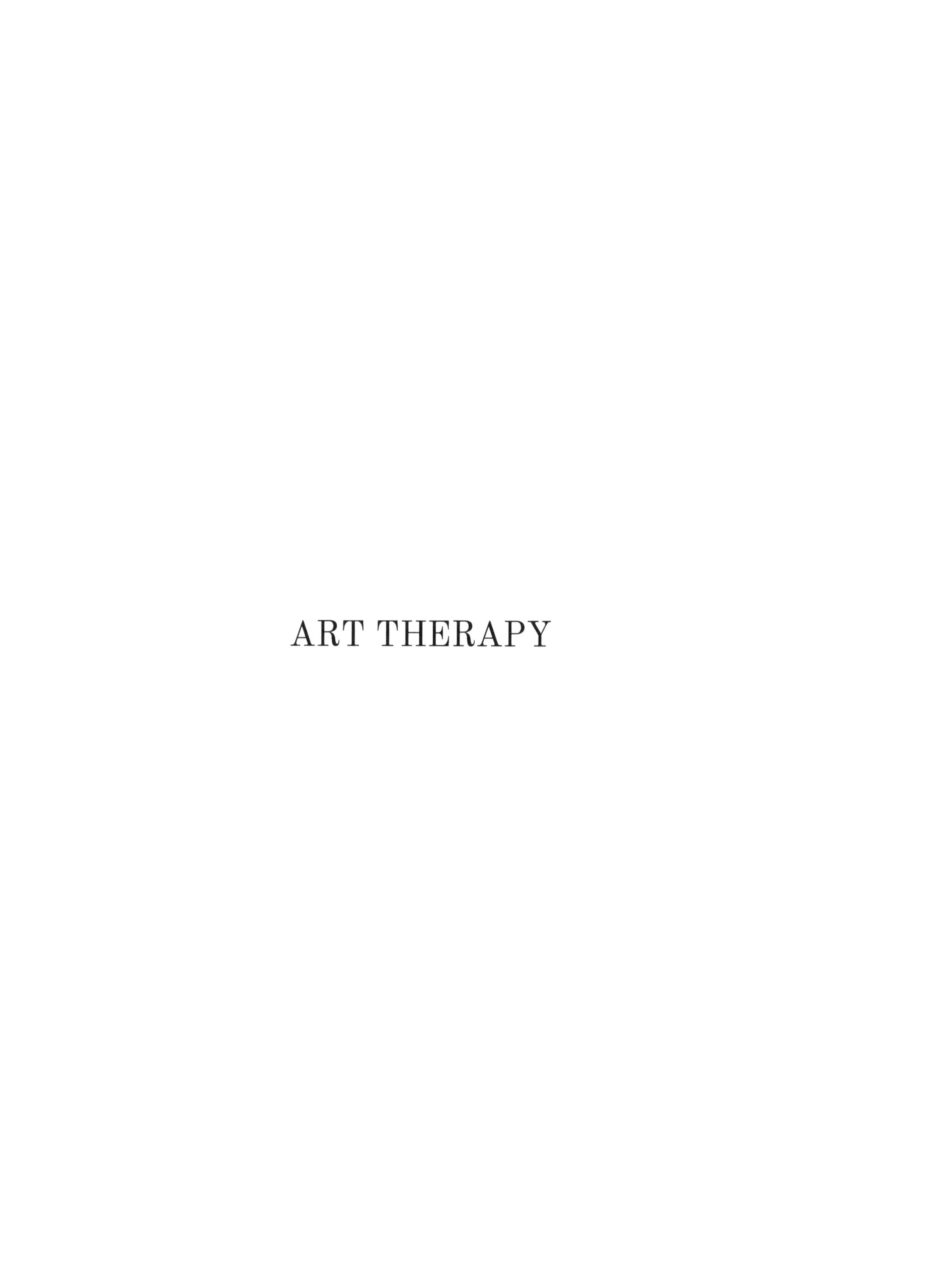

ART THERAPY

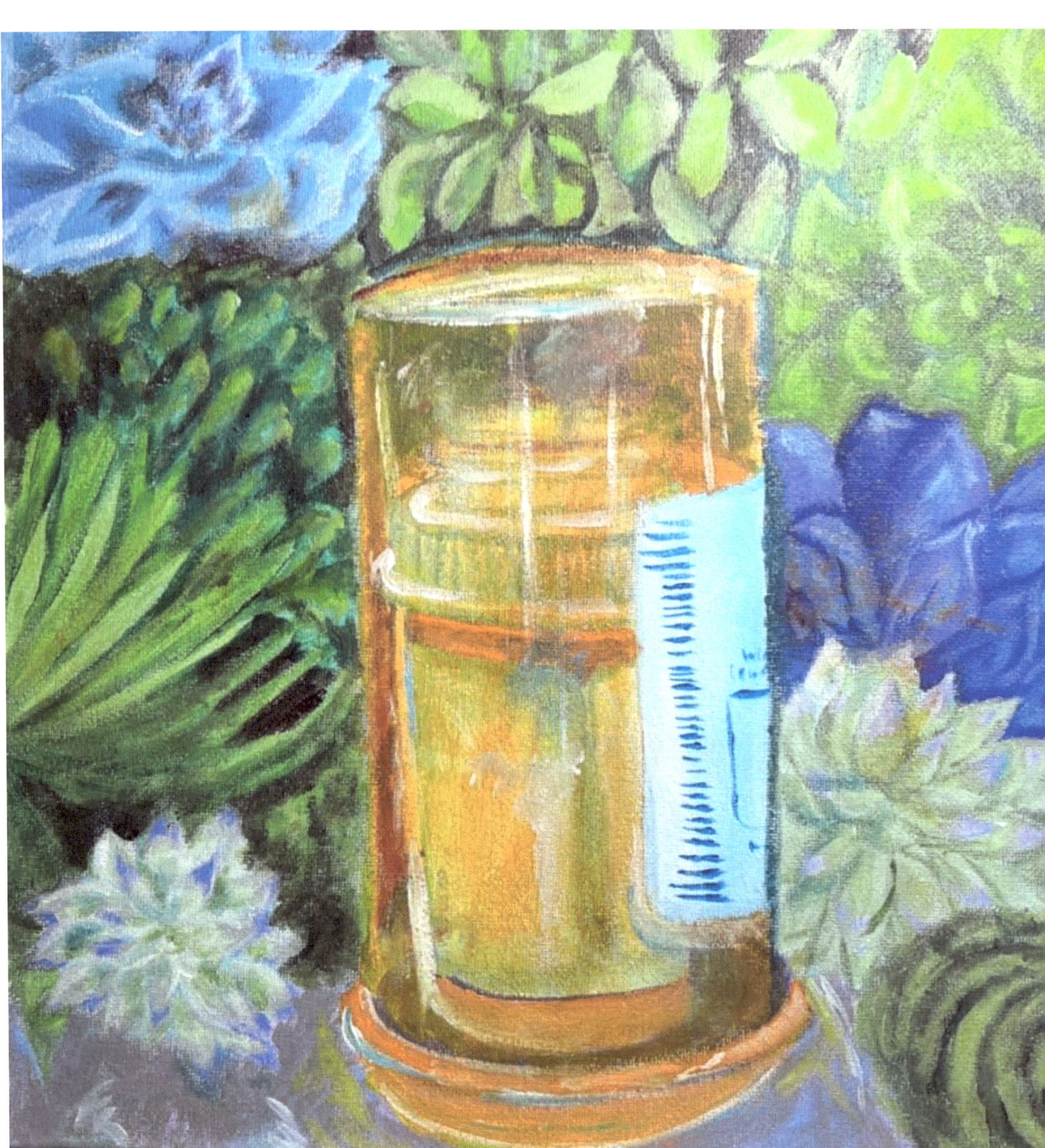

It can often be difficult to put emotions into words, especially if you are conditioned to not share your emotions with fear of retaliation. Research proposes that women survivors of intimate partner violence have difficulty with talk therapies due to past abuse (Binkley 2013). When I first got out of the relationship, I did not know how to navigate talking to a therapist about it. In fact, I stopped going to therapy because of it.

In a study published in the International Journey of Art Therapy in 2022, "six women were interviewed about their experiences of participating in a 12-week GAT program within a Canadian domestic violence prevention agency, (with) the overarching theme of transformative healing, which women appeared to experience by creating connections in a safe space, using visual metaphors in their art-pieces, reclaiming an empowered self, and building resilience" (Skop, Darewych, Root & Mason 2022).

Transformative healing is a major theme in working with survivors of sexual assault and intimate partner violence. It can be guided, but is truly found internally through therapeutic processes, especially within art therapy. With my experience leading art workshops with survivors of sexual assault and domestic violence, as well as those who struggle with general trauma, it is a healing that can begin to show through quickly, from hours to months. Even within myself, the time period of four months entrenching myself into art as a therapy and coping skill, I gained a renewed sense of confidence, empowerment, and safety. "The artwork products record the therapeutic process" (Woollett, Bandeira, & Hatcher 2020); which feels good as the patient, because you can see your progress.

While progress is not linear, it can encourage hope of healing, step by step. While one will never fully be able to erase trauma, healing can look like getting up and taking a shower everyday. It is truly the little things we take for granted, until we are in a place that we cannot do them. Even now, sometimes the only reason I get out of bed and take a shower is to go paint.

Therapy, especially talk therapy, is not accessible to everyone. With many barriers, such as financial inequities, generational trauma with healthcare (especially in marginalized communities), therapist shortages, and more, it is more difficult than ever before. Art therapy groups are becoming more accessible from non profits, educational institutions, and shelters. With relatively affordable supplies, even just having a piece of paper and a pencil, art is a form of therapy that can be practiced on the go.

Art therapy can be very personal, but overall it is a community thing. Art therapy is often done in groups, especially among survivors of intimate partner violence, due to the isolation that many feel (Woollett, Bandeira, & Hatcher 2020). The community surrounding the art therapy is equally as important as creating the artwork itself, because being a survivor of abuse is isolating, and to know that there are others out there that will understand you and not just pity you, is fulfilling.

Art therapy allows someone to express their emotions, but lets them talk when they are ready. The works made through art therapy create a dialogue between viewer and artist, and allow a space for both to feel empowered. Empowerment is a great energy source for healing, as it feels like you can take control of your own narrative back, despite the stigmas and labels others stick on to you.

There is so much potential in creating accessibility to mental healthcare assistance, building communities, encouraging empowerment and breaking stigmas. Art has been such a staple across all cultures for communication and expression, so why not take advantage of cross disciplinary solutions into our fields of science and humanities?

AN ART GALLERY TRIP
BEFORE WE SAY
GOODBYE.

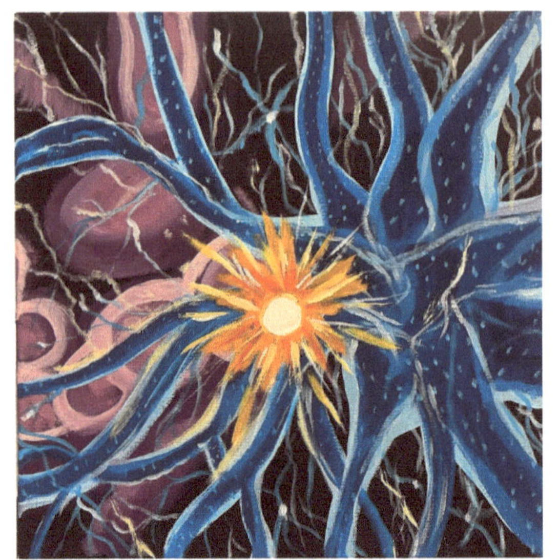

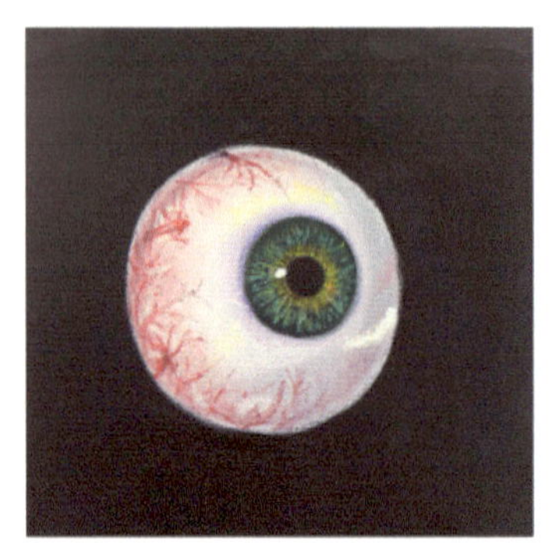

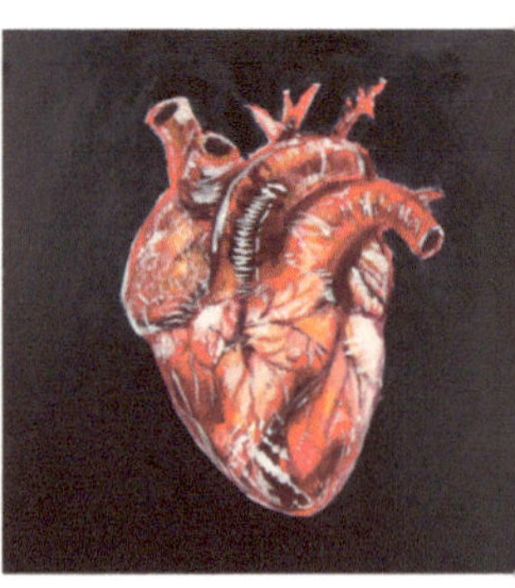

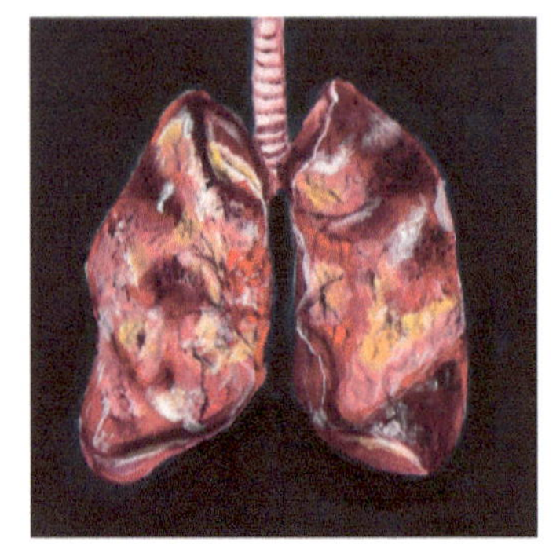

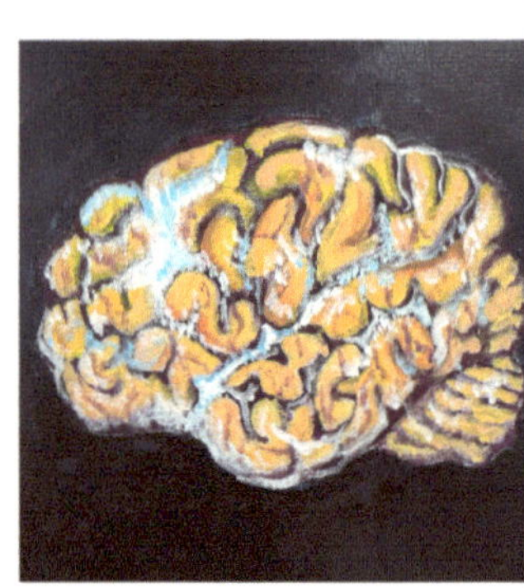

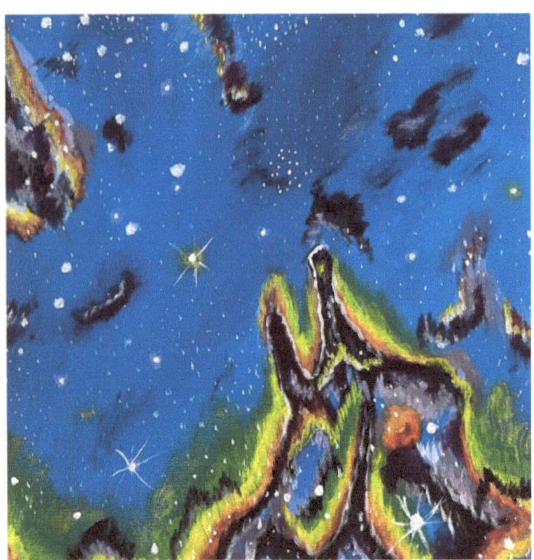

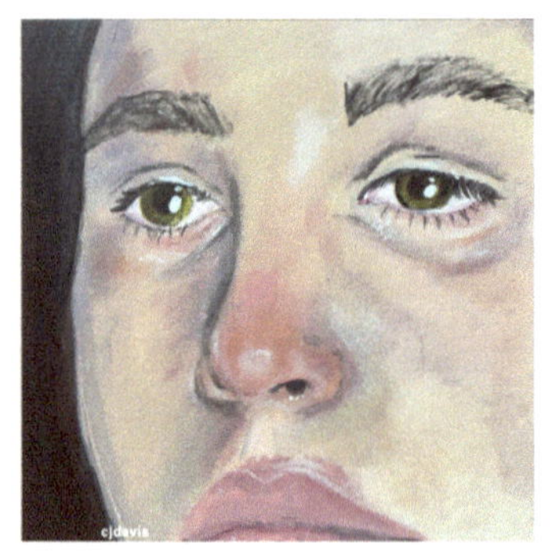
cjdavis

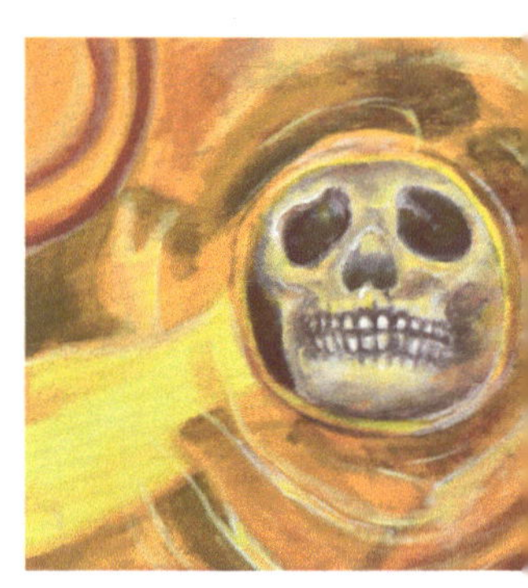

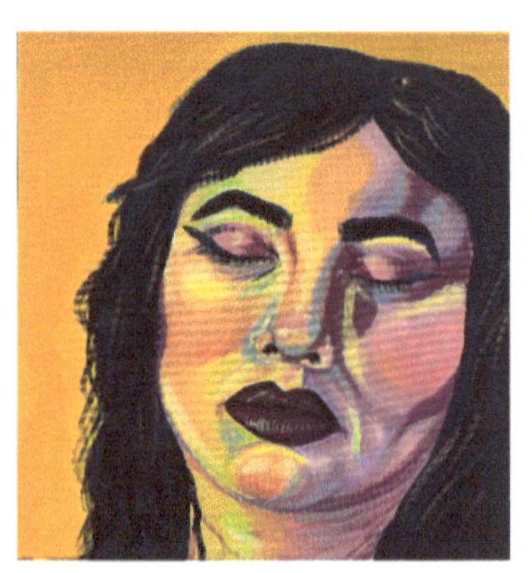

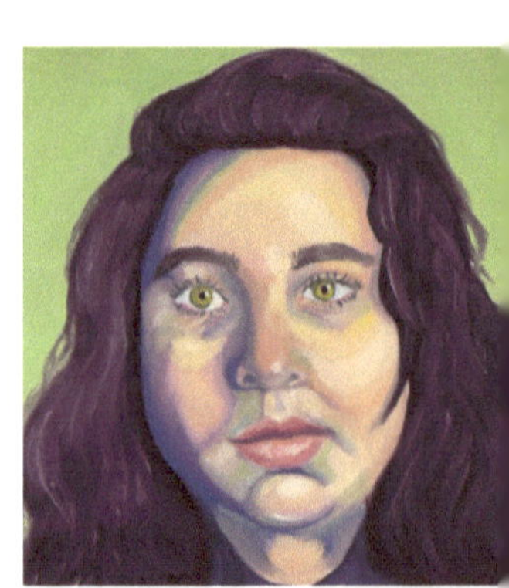

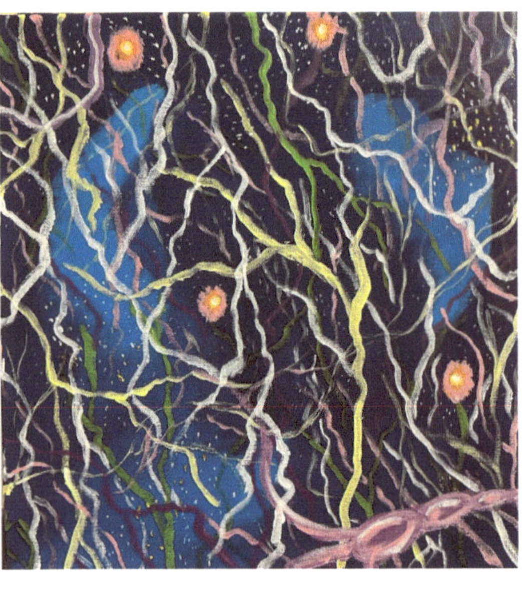

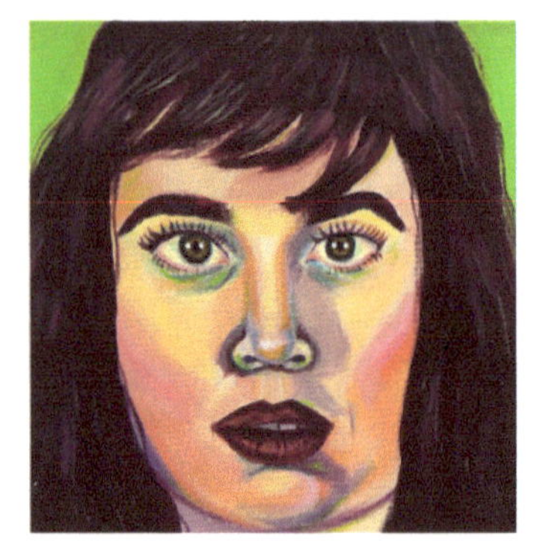

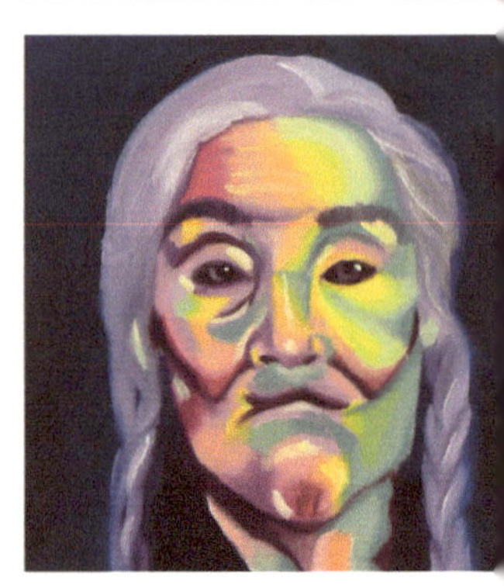

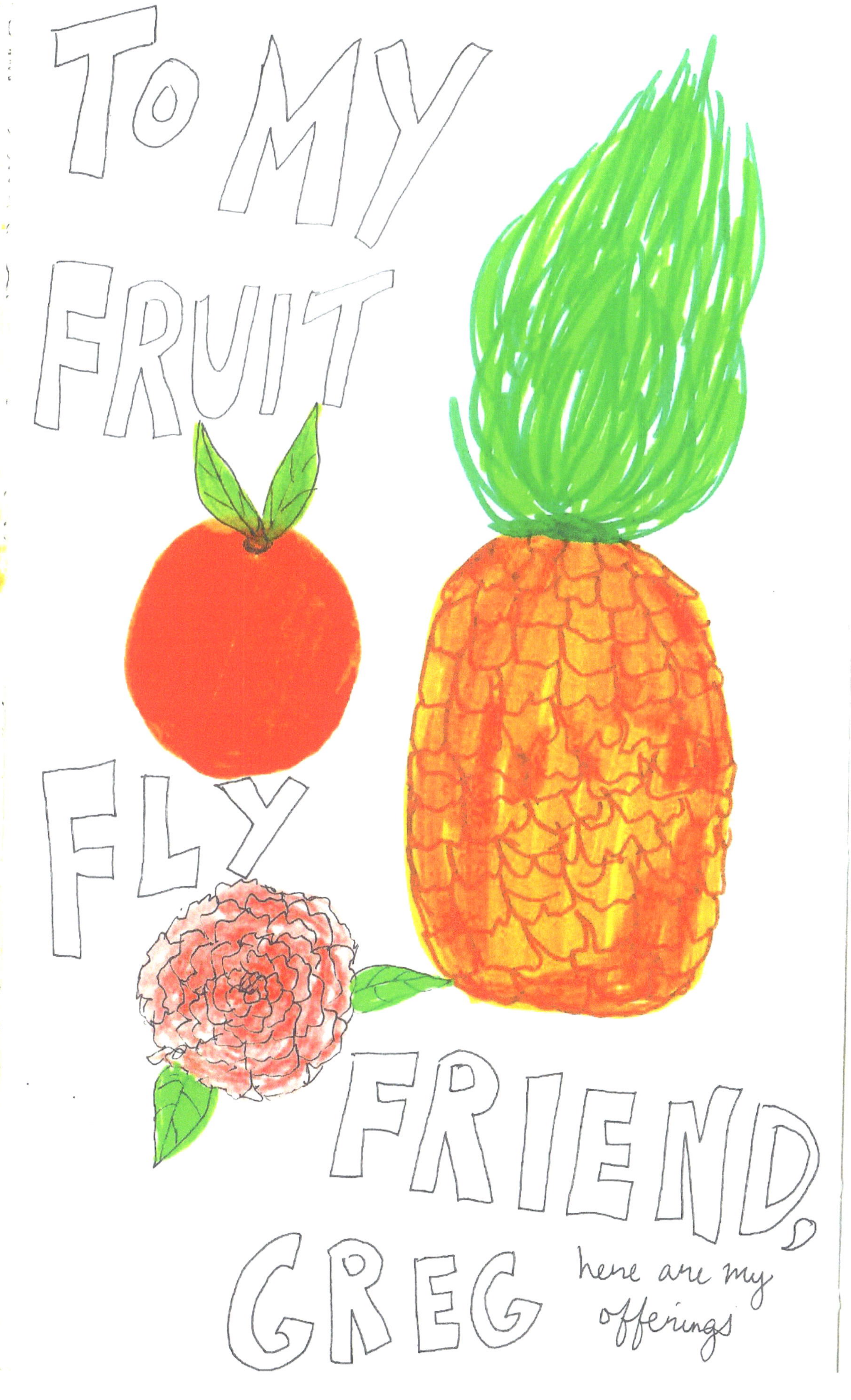

TO MY FRUIT FLY FRIEND, GREG

here are my offerings

To my little friend I accidentally squished,

I'm sorry, I swear I didn't mean to
Now your tiny bug blood is smeared across this page
and your life is soaked through the fine tooth of moleskine paper
You were just looking for the light, and I sent you to the wrong one.

Ever Yours,
CJ

RIP TO MY FRUIT FLY FRIEND, GREG

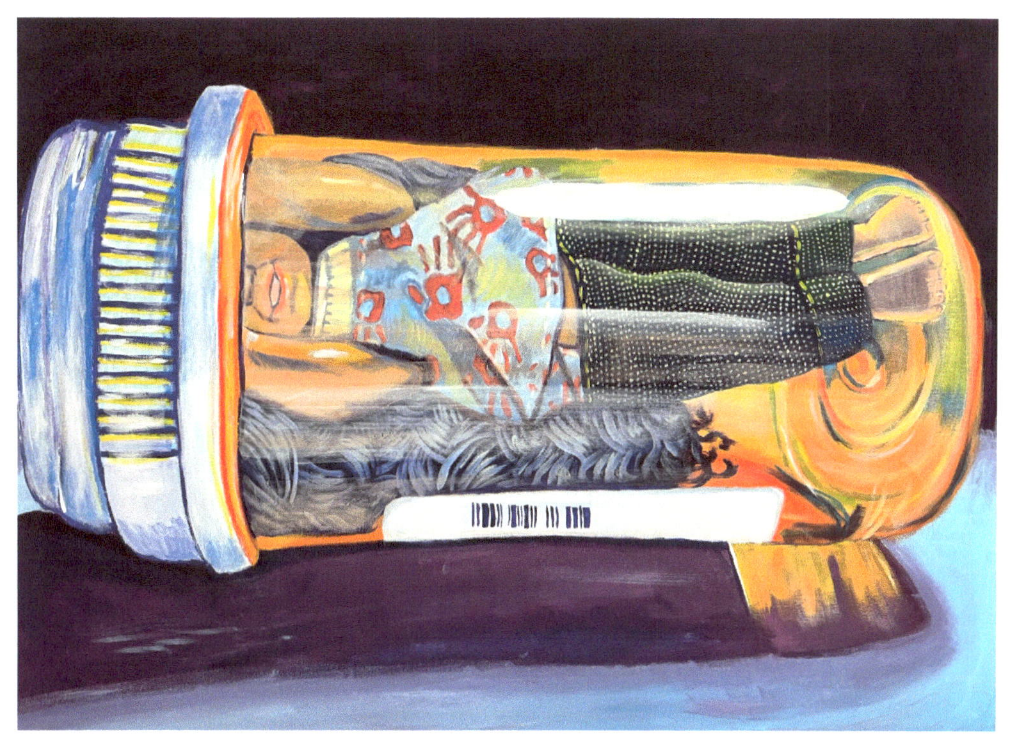

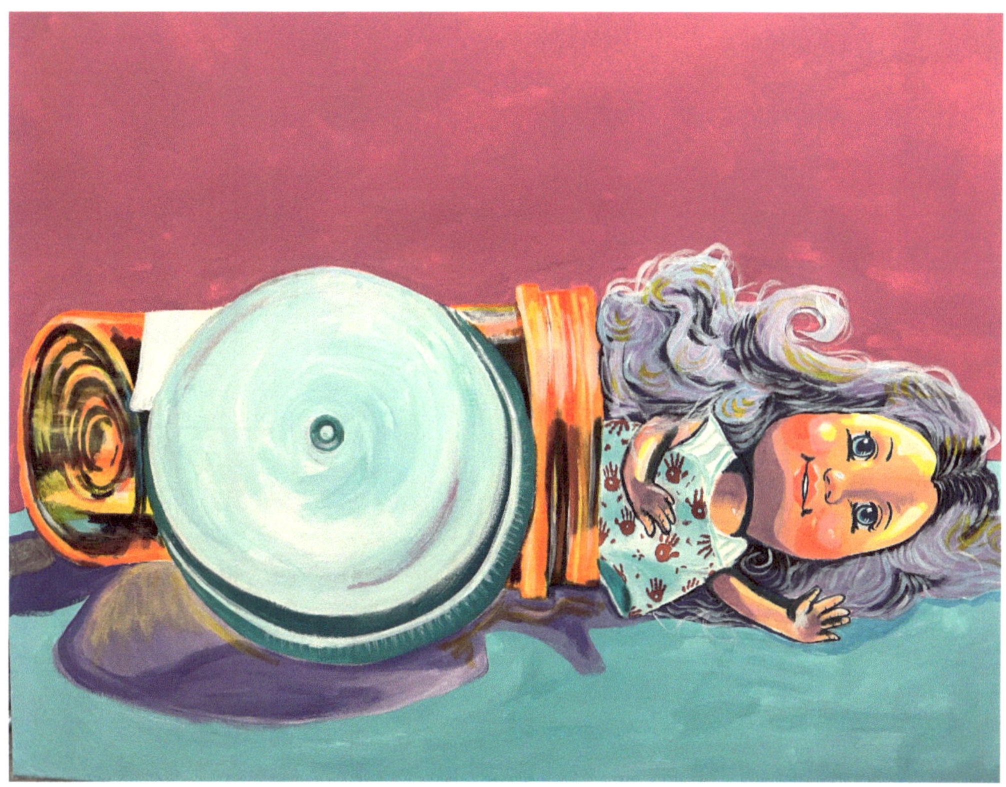

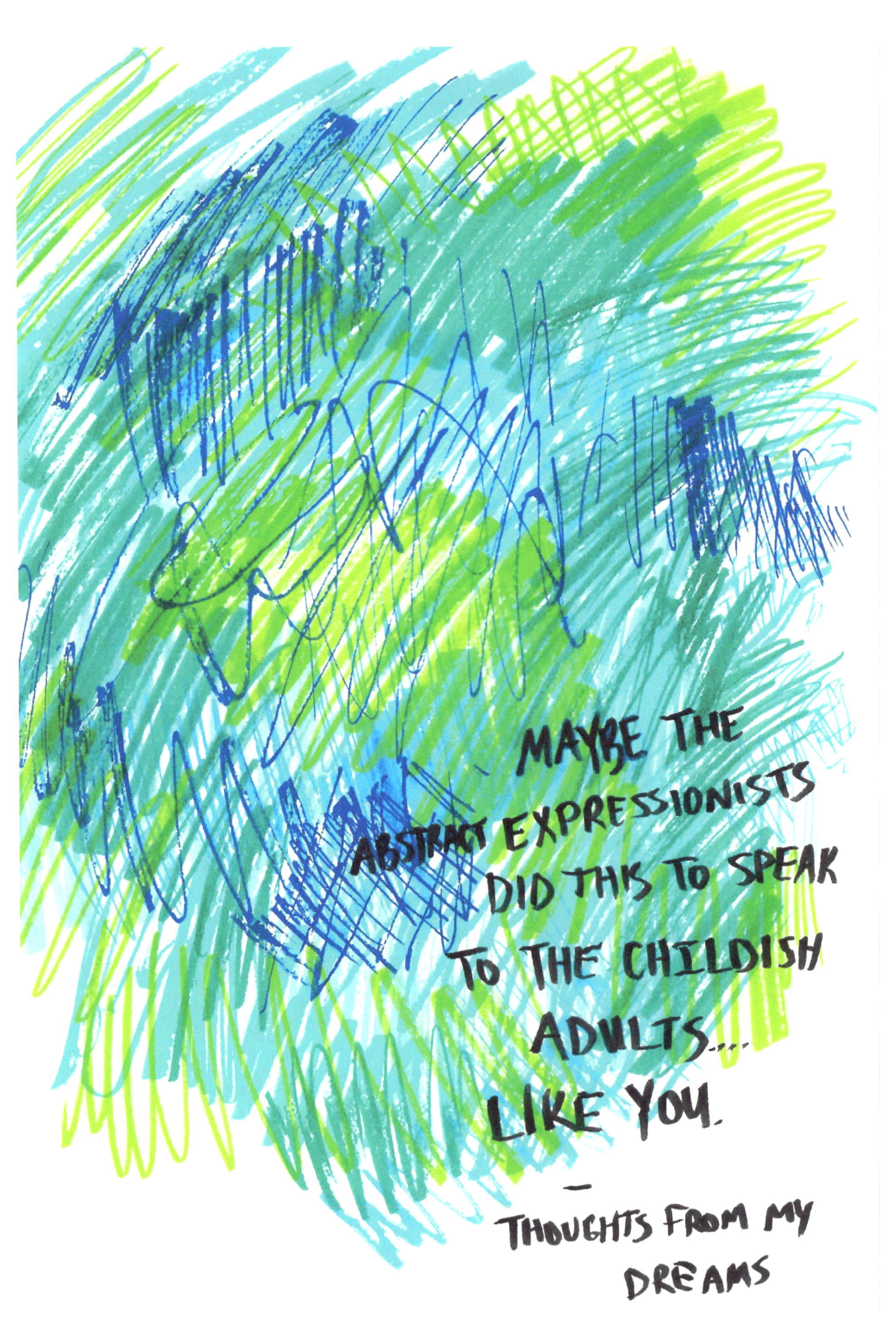
MAYBE THE
ABSTRACT EXPRESSIONISTS
DID THIS TO SPEAK
TO THE CHILDISH
ADULTS....
LIKE YOU.
- THOUGHTS FROM MY
DREAMS

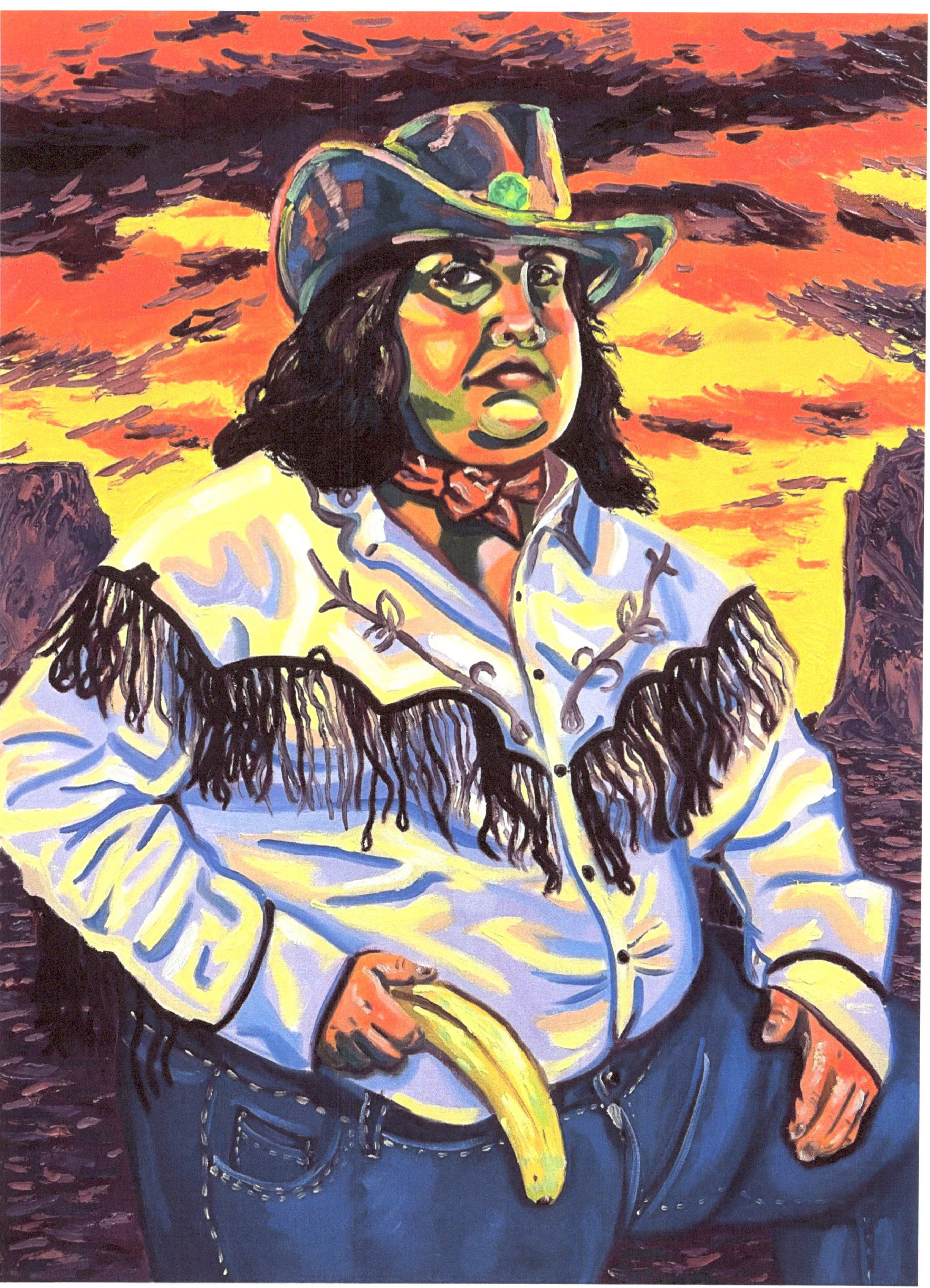

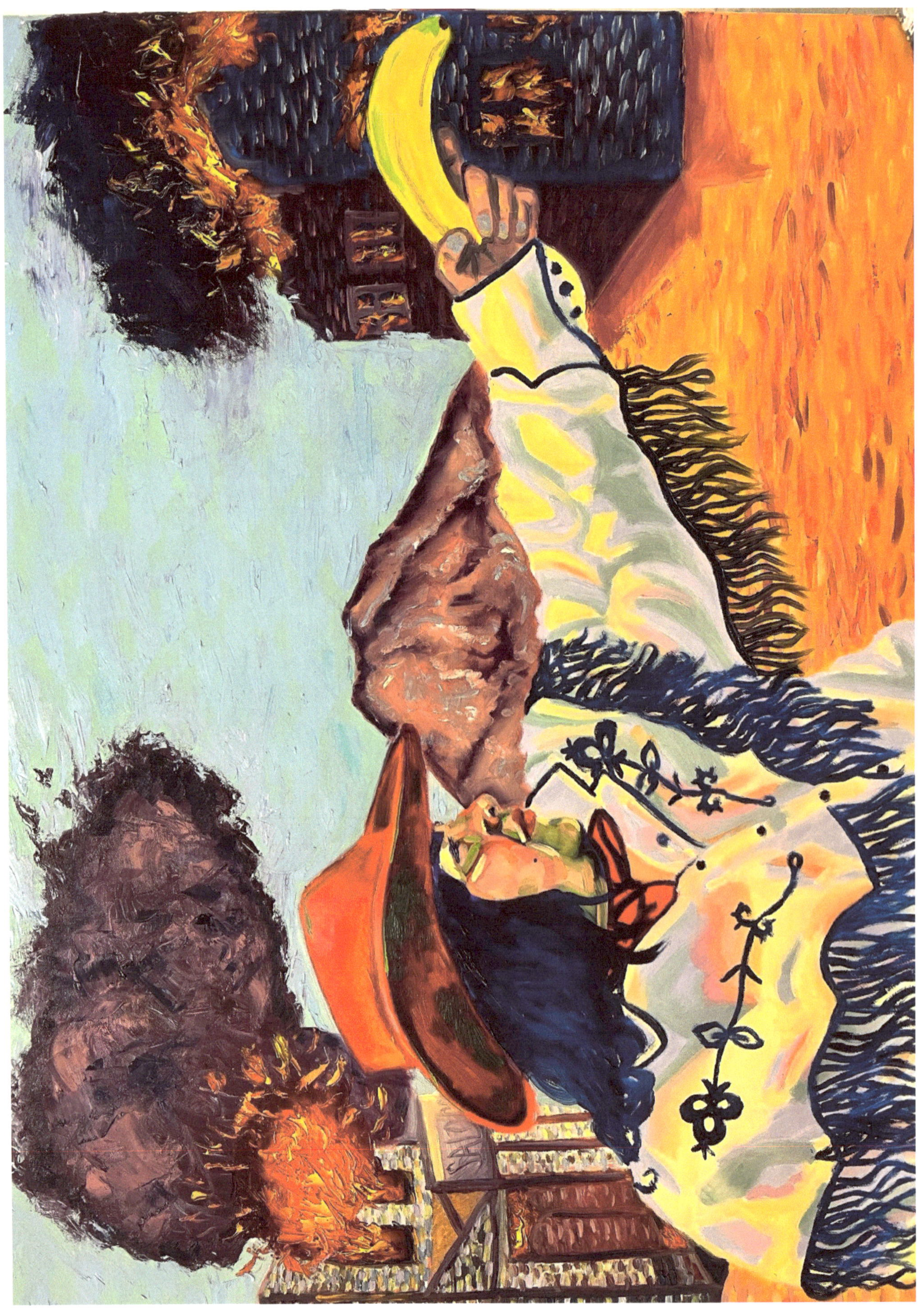

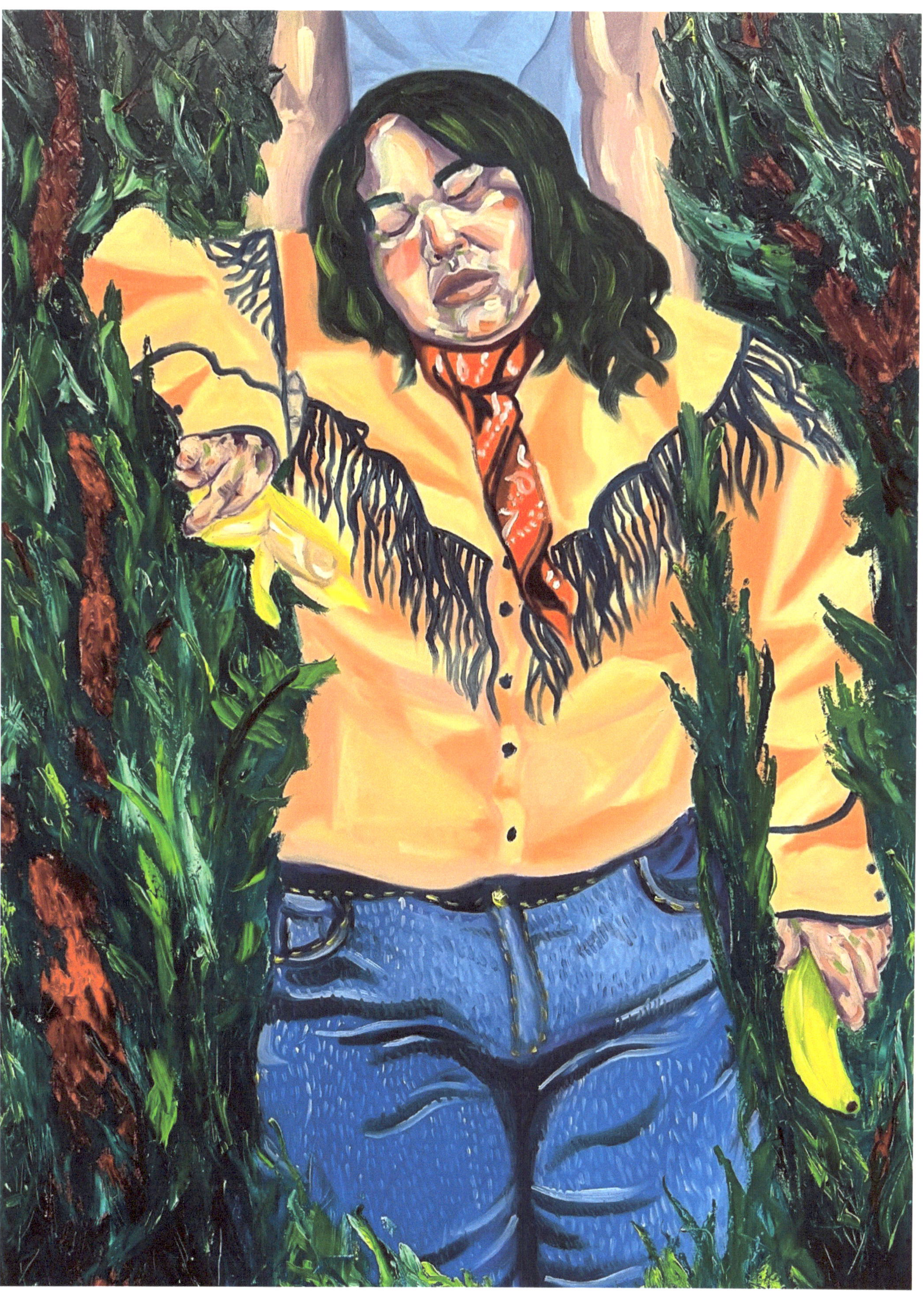

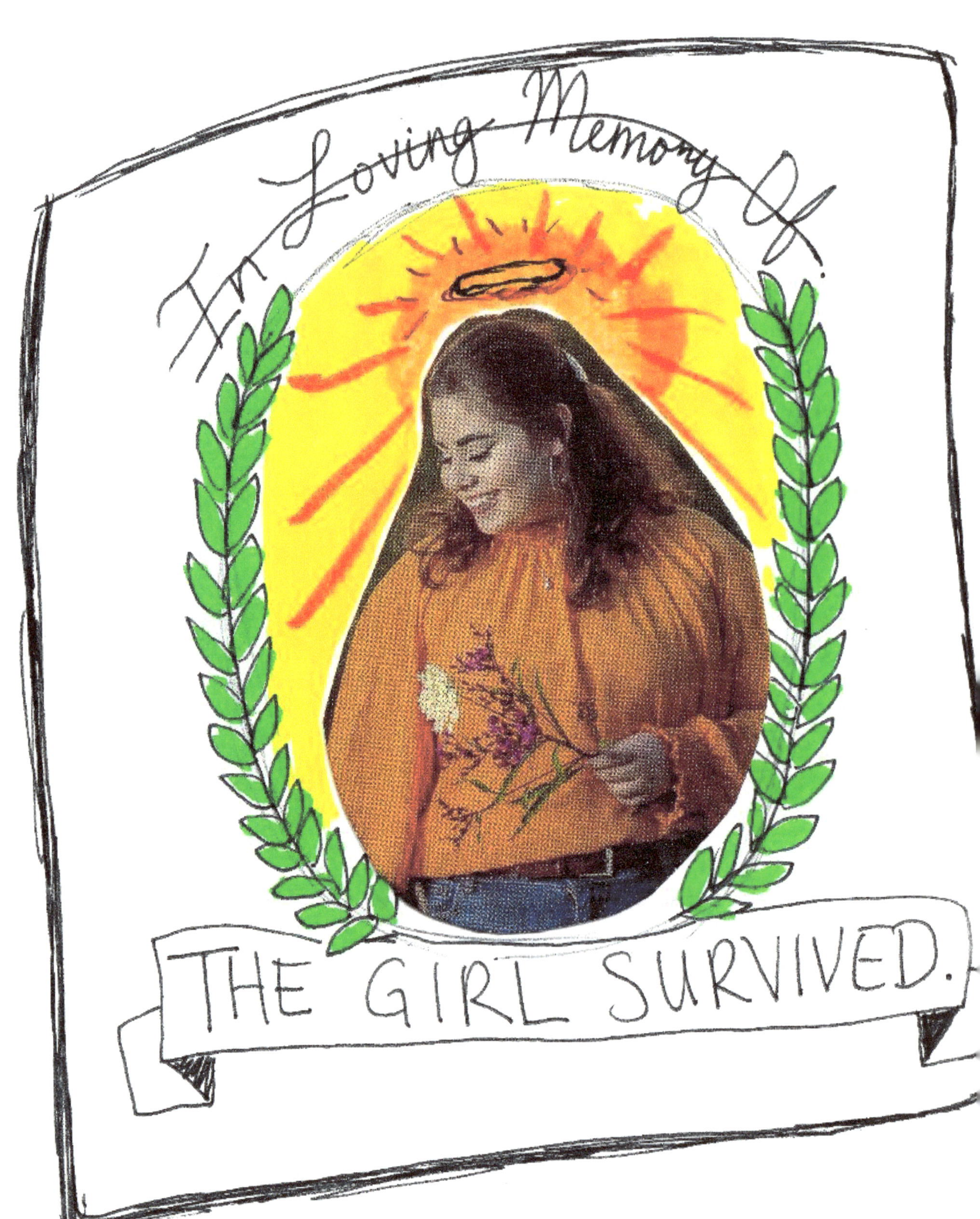
In Loving Memory Of:
THE GIRL SURVIVED.

RETURN TO ROOTS.

My return to my roots was a harrowing process, and I made it through by taking established support and creating new support groups. I could not have done it with the people in my life following the next two years after the relationship, and there are still more years to come. The two year anniversary of the attempt on my life was ironically on Easter, a few weeks before I finished this book to publish, but I did not think too much of it that day. I spent time with my family, talked to my friends, and celebrated my life.

I feel like returning to my art, my writing, rebuilding relationships with my family and my friends, and creating community in the different spaces I am a part of has made me feel like I am the best version of myself that I could ask for at this moment in time. I've had so many opportunities come up to share my art in exhibitions, do public speaking events, community outreaches and more since returning to what I love: art.

After so much loss, the lack of confidence in myself and my intelligence, I have recovered these things. While I still feel pain, have post traumatic stress episodes, anxiety, and more, I am able to root myself in my beliefs, stay grounded with coping through art and writing, and know that there are people that care.

It is valid to feel anger about the people that didn't save you, even if they were strangers. It still sucks to know that the people that you thought were your original roots simply left. It is rage-inducing to be pitied and reduced to just a "victim." It is easy to spiral into feeling completely isolated because people may never understand what you went through, and the lasting effects. Especially when the effects are simple things, like breathing comfortably in your sleep.

I will never be the person I was before the abuse. I still resent that many days. However, returning to my art and writing in such a strong return has validated me that I am back on the path to pursue my dreams. Even if art isn't your thing, there are so many healthy outlets out there to cope, to find opportunity, and to find strength when it is hard to find.

If there is anything that you can take away from this book, I want you to feel seen. I want you to know you are not alone. No matter what you are struggling with. There are people out there for you. For the friends and family of those struggling, you will never fully understand the pain and journey, but your unconditional love and support, even if it is just sitting in silence with someone- is the greatest gift you could give. For the academic and health professionals reading this, I hope you can find humanity within statistics and studies.

What will you return to? Where do your roots lie? What foundation will keep you grounded?

You will rise again.

THE GREATEST
COMPLIMENT I COULD
EVER RECIEVE IS THAT
I AM A GREAT STORYTELLER.
IT IS ALL I HAVE TO
OFFER.

GOODNIGHT, FROM 4AM
MUSINGS, EMPTY PIBB
CAN, DIRTY GLASSES AND
A TOUCH OF MANIA.

ACKNOWLEDGEMENTS

First and foremost, I would like to thank the Undergraduate Research Scholars Program award from the Office of Student Scholarship, Creative Activities, and Research at George Mason University for funding this project and publication.

I would like to give a tremendous thank you to my mentor, Heather Green for supporting me, giving me feedback, helping me grow as a writer, helping me gain confidence and my love of writing back. I could not have done this without you.

I would like to acknowledge my professor, Chawky Frenn, for being my painting mentor. He often speaks about painting coming from the "fire in your belly" and using art as a vehicle for change and empowerment. He has pushed me to become a better artist, and I am forever grateful for his authenticity and guidance.

I would like to thank my parents, Tony and Cindy Davis, for supporting my artistic endeavors since I was young. My father taught me how to read and encouraged education as a form of empowerment. My mother encouraged my writing, as she would always read my scribbled stories in endless composition notebooks. Both of them showed me the love of life and people, how to lead, and teach me the values that I will cling on to forever.

I would like to thank my siblings, Amelia and John, who have been alongside me in the journey. John reminded me to indent my paragraphs, which really helped.

I would like to thank my uncle Wayne, who listened to my ramblings on the phone for hours, encouraging me consistently and giving me reassurance.

I would like to thank my aunt Dee, who is one of the strongest women I know. She has continued to spark my interest in mental healthcare, and was one of the first artists I knew growing up.

I would like to thank my lifelong best friend, Shannon and her family. Without them, I would not be who I am today, inspired by the passion of music, writing, and the arts. Shannon has been my rock and has always listened to me intently without judgment.

I would like to thank my best friend since high school, Matt. I call him whenever I feel sad, and even just hearing his voice, I feel better. He has been one of the most consistent people in my life, and I always know he is there. He is my concert buddy, my adventure buddy, my sports game buddy, and one of the best friends I could ever ask for.

I would like to thank Jojo, and I appreciate their consistent and unconditional love and support throughout everything. They always are able to be genuine and honest with me throughout the years I have known them. I have so much respect and love of their brilliance and light.

I would like to thank Vinh, my first friend I made in college. Our sassy natures collided and the world has never been the same. His support, love, sass, and good food keeps me going.

I would like to thank PJ. Even though we are not in a relationship anymore, I am so grateful for his friendship and kindness. He encouraged me to return to my roots and return to art. Our long conversations about music and art will always stick to my core, and has given me a much deeper appreciation for music. I appreciate him for letting me sleep on his couch when I was deeply afraid, and for letting me feel human again.

I would like to thank my sorority sisters, especially Shelby, Anna, Dima, Amanda, Megan and Elisabeth. I am grateful for their support and love. I love being able to connect with them after having more time to rebuild and strengthen my friendships.

I would like to thank my dear friend Guinevere, who I have met recently, but has been one of the people who truly understands my emotions, and me. She is one of the best artists I know, and she inspires me to push my limits in painting- sometimes without her even knowing. Our friendship blossomed so quickly, and she is a light in my life.

I would like to thank my dear art studio friends, especially Pat and David. Pat has been such a positive person in my life, and he makes sure I drink water and breathe- which can be a daunting task when I only drink ice coffee all day. David has been so encouraging, and I know if something were to happen to me, I could call him any time of the day and he will be there.

Finally, I would like to thank the people in my life in every connection possible, from different communities, to connections through organizations, and school. I have so much love for everyone in my life, and I feel that everyone has made me who I am today, and I will be forever grateful for the support of my craft. I feel like I can be the best version of myself in this moment of time, and I strive to feel better and be better as time goes on.

REFERENCES

Erin Binkley (2013) Creative Strategies for Treating Victims of Domestic Violence, Journal of Creativity in Mental Health, 8:3, 305-313, DOI: 10.1080/15401383.2013.821932

Michelle Skop, Olena Helen Darewych, Jennifer Root & Julie Mason (2022) Exploring intimate partner violence survivors' experiences with group art therapy, International Journal of Art Therapy, 27:4, 159-168, DOI: 10.1080/17454832.2022.2124298

Overstreet, N. M., & Quinn, D. M. (2013). The Intimate Partner Violence Stigmatization Model and Barriers to Help-Seeking. *Basic and applied social psychology*, *35*(1), 109–122. https://doi.org/10.1080/01973533.2012.746599

Woollett, N., Bandeira, M., & Hatcher, A. (2020). Trauma-informed art and play therapy: Pilot study outcomes for children and mothers in domestic violence shelters in the United States and South Africa. *Child abuse & neglect*, *107*, 104564. https://doi.org/10.1016/j.chiabu.2020.104564

ABOUT THE AUTHOR

CJ Davis is a Mexican-American painter living in Northern Virginia. She is currently a BFA student concentrating in InterArts at George Mason University's School of Art. CJ loves to spend time with her loving family, her cat, Penny, her dog, Pepper, her friends, and communities in the area.

When she is not painting, she is heavily involved in advocacy work. She is passionate about advocacy work involving immigration and healthcare (especially mental health care) equity and policy and the support of sexual assault and domestic violence survivors, as well as marginalized communities.

In 2021, she was chosen to deliver a TEDx talk at George Mason University, addressing a lack of diversity in the art world, and working toward equity. “Art Looks Better in Color” is her breakout TEDx talk. In 2022, Davis was chosen to do a second TEDx talk, “Hurting Hearts to Hear and Heal,” a personal narrative about the struggles with mental illness in marginalized communities, and how she healed through art. She has facilitated art workshops, given media interviews, and taught classes in local libraries in Northern Virginia, all on the subject of art and healing.

www.ingramcontent.com/pod-product-compliance
Lightning Source LLC
Chambersburg PA
CBHW041642110726
48005CB00003B/683

* 9 7 9 8 2 1 8 1 7 9 9 2 2 *